Rev. Charles William Turner

Annals of St. John's Church, Huntington, Suffolk County, N.Y.

Also historical and descriptive notes

.

Rev. Charles William Turner

Annals of St. John's Church, Huntington, Suffolk County, N.Y.
Also historical and descriptive notes

ISBN/EAN: 9783337261108

Printed in Europe, USA, Canada, Australia, Japan

Cover: Foto ©Lupo / pixelio.de

More available books at **www.hansebooks.com**

Annals

of

St. John's Church,

Huntington,

Suffolk County, N. Y.

Also,

Historical and Descriptive Notes.

Edited by

Rev. Chas. Wm. Turner,

Rector

The Stiles Printing House, Hunton, Co. N. Y.

1897

CONTENTS:

PREFACE.

The writing of a preface to a book to be published without an index may be regarded as but an aggravation of a serious fault.

But the preface can be confined to the space available :— an index, to be worth anything, must be made complete. And as this book though not large, has already grown to a length considerably beyond the estimate in number of pages, it is hoped that the table of contents hereto appended, may serve all ordinary requirements of reference.

The writer is indebted to his predecessors, not only for valuable material and notes, but also for the very idea of the work. To those in particular, who in succession immediately preceeded him, the Rev. N. Barrows and the Rev. Theo. M. Peck, he is thus indebted. Yet he might scarcely have set himself seriously to the labor involved in the fulfilment of the purpose, which they had had in mind, or have ventured to count upon sufficient support to justify the publication, but for the kind encouragement and aid given by friends among the laity, and in particular by Mr. O. Egerton Schmidt, Mr. Temple Prime and Miss Cornelia Prime. The former, indeed, of his own motion, had prepared for publication a " List of Rectors" with dates, intending to present copies to his fellow parishioners. He submitted the proof sheet of this to the writer for revision, and readily approved the latter's suggestion that a few notes might be added.

The few notes have gradually grown, through many additions, corrections and rearrangements to the present work, in the progress of which as well as in the details attending publication the other kind friends named have taken a deep and encouraging interest.

The various manuscripts and publications drawn upon have been indicated in the text. The writer will gladly receive, and carefully preserve, any communications in regard to matters left undetermined or incorrectly stated, and also any additions to our scanty stock of material. He trusts that what his 'prentice hand has been able to set forth may be acceptable and interesting to his readers, and may perhaps prepare the way for a fuller and better story of the struggles and progress of this ancient parish by some one among his successors.

Ascension Day,   C. W. T.
    May 23d, 1895.

THE Episcopal Church in Huntington or, as it was then called, the Church of England, was planted by Missionaries of the Church of England "Society for the Propagation" "of the Gospel," stationed at Hempstead, in Queens County. Their acts and missionary efforts are recorded in the Parish Register of St. George's Church in that place. From that register, an extract of Baptisms, Marriages, &c., relating to Huntington, was made on the 3d Sunday in August, 1846, by the Rev. Chas. H. Hall, D.D., of Holy Trinity Church, Brooklyn, then rector of this parish.

From the compilation above mentioned it appears that the first official act of which there is record was the marriage here on August 25th, 1727, of Benj. Treadwell, of Hempstead, and Phœbe Platt, of Huntington, by the Rev. Robert Jenney, of Hempstead, the first Missionary whose acts are on record in the Parish Register of St. George's Church.

But this one ministerial act seems to have been simply incidental to Mr. Jenney's work at Hempstead. The first missionary there who made frequent visits and who put forth the effort which resulted in the building of a church and the gathering of a congregation was his successor, the REV. SAMUEL SEABURY, settled at Hempstead from August, 1742, to June, 1764. It will be seen from the following record that beginning with the year 1744, that honored Missionary visited Huntington from time to time, baptized a number of persons, both children and adults, and was evidently so earnest in his efforts

that a church building, begun probably in 1747, was completed
and in use in 1750, and that his son, Samuel Seabury, Jr., the
future first Bishop of the American Church, was ministering
therein, having been commissioned by the "Society for the
Propagation of the Gospel" to serve as Catechist or Lay-
Reader.

A. D. 1744. In this year, the Rev. Samuel Seabury visited Huntington, and on June 21st baptized Mary Bryan,
daughter of John and Elizabeth Bryan. This is the first baptism on record.

June 23d. Thomas Keble, of Oyster Bay, writes to the Secretary of the Society for the Propagation of the Gospel :

"Since Mr. Seabury came, " (*i. e.* to Hempstead) "he has
"visited and preached upon week days, and has roused them
"up in all quarters of his parish, amongst all the denominations
"and others, particularly in this place " (Oyster Bay) " where
"I now live. " He has preached three times upon week-days,
"besides several visits, and has baptised children of four fami-
"lies, and one adult. " .... " And of late he has preached at
"Huntington, an old Independent place within five miles of
"Oyster Bay church, being invited by some of the people there
"who of late came constantly to church at Oyster Bay, and
"sometimes to Hempstead : for the Independent and voluntary
"preachers have infused false notions into the people of these
"parts of the discipline of the Church of England, particularly
"of the Liturgy, which Mr. Seabury takes pains to explain at
"all reasonable times." (Note by Mr. Henry Onderdonk, from
copies of the S. P. G. papers, Dr. Hawks, Mss. ii, 168.)

A. D. 1745. This year is given, in the list of parishes appended to the Journals of the Diocesan Conventions, as the "date of organization" of this parish.

A. D. 1746. February 3d. Three baptisms by Rev. Samuel Seabury. (For names, &c,, see entries in Parish Register, copied from the Parish Register of St. George's, Hempstead.)

July 24th. Two baptisms by the Rev. Samuel Seabury. (For names, &c., see entries, &c.)

A. D. 1747. March 18th. Two baptisms by Rev. S. Seabury. (For names, &c., see entries, &c.)

A. D. 1748. "In 1748 Mr. Seabury informed the Society "that at Huntington, a town about 18 miles distant from "Hempstead, a considerable number of people had conformed, "and built a Church for the worship of God according to the "Liturgy of the Church of England : that he had frequently "officiated there ; and that, at their requests, his son, who had "been educated at New Haven, read prayers and sermons, "under his direction. Such being the case, he requested that "his son, who would be recommended by the Commissary "might be appointed by the Society to be a Catechist, with "some small allowance. The Society accordingly appointed "Mr. Samuel Seabury, Junior, to act in this capacity, under "the direction of his father, and allowed him a salary of £10 a "year." (Extract from Hawkins' Colonial History, Note No. 1 in Parish Register.)

August 3d. Three baptisms by Rev. Samuel Seabury, one being at Eaton's Neck. (For names, &c., see entries, &c.)

September 30th.   One baptism.   (See, &c.)

It is stated in the foregoing note that in 1748 Mr. Seabury informed the Society that people in Huntington had conformed "and built a Church." It is not easy to reconcile this with certain expressions in a "preamble and resolutions" which follow, under date of "September, 1749," unless, indeed, the correct date should be September, 1747.

The Secretary of the S. P. G. has kindly verified Canon Hawkins' statement by sending the following extracts from the original documents :

I.   Extract from a letter of Rev. Samuel Seabury to the Society :

"HEMPSTEAD, September 30th, 1748.

"REVEREND SIR :

*   *   *   I embrace this opportunity to lay before "the Society the state of Huntington, a town about eighteen "miles distant from Hempstead : where a number of people "have conformed to the Established religion and have built a "Church for the worship of GOD according to our Lyturgie.

*   *   *   *   *   *   *   *

"SAMUEL SEABURY."

II.   Extract from

"The Humble address of the inhabitants of Huntington "(on Long Island, in New York Province) and places adjacent, "to the Honorable Society, &c.   *   *   *

"We have most heartily embraced the Established Church "....In our zeal for which we have Built a Church, that in a "little time will be commodious for Publick use.   *   *   *   *

"HUNTINGTON, Sep. 30th, 1748."

These extracts are conclusive evidence that by Sep. 30th, 1748, some building or part of a building described as "a Church" had been erected; but the concluding sentence of the "Humble Address" seems to indicate that it had not been completed, and apparently, that it would need not only furnishing but also enlargement to make it "commodious for publick use."

This request of the Rev. S. Seabury for the appointment of his son as Catechist was accompanied by a petition from the Churchmen of Huntington to the Venerable Society :—from which the following is an extract :

"We are inhabitants of a town which till of late, has been "under great prejudices to the Church of England, a few ex-"cepted: but by late enthusiastic confusions,* which mightily "prevailed here, some of us have been awakened to consider "the consequences of those principles in which we have been "educated, and by the assistance of the Reverend Mr. Sea-"bury, the Society's Missionary at Hempstead, who has been "very ready to visit us on week days, and to perform divine "service among us, we have most heartily embraced the estab-"lished Church, and think it our duty, for our own improve-"ment in true religion, for the good of our country, and for "the honour of God, to join with our neighbours, conformists, "and do all in our power for the promotion of the interests of "the established Church : in our zeal for which, we "have built a church, that, in a little time, will be com-"modious for public use : but as we are eighteen miles distant

---

* The reference here is to some revival excitement. Rev. N. S. Prime mentions a "general awakening" in 1741 : a note by the late Dr. Moore, of Hempstead, mentions "Whitfield's orations."

"from Mr. Seabury, who is the nearest Missionary, and he
"being obliged to attend two churches in his own parish, viz. :
"those of Hempstead and Oyster Bay, we therefore most
"humbly beg the Society to attend to our prayers, which is
"that Mr. Samuel Seabury, the son of your worthy Missionary,
"a young gentleman (lately educated and graduated at Yale
"College) of a good character and excellent hopes, may be ap-
"pointed the Society's Catechist at this place, and perform
"divine service among us in a lay capacity, with some allow-
"ance from the Honourable Society for that service.

"In testimony of our sincerity, we have to this affixed our
"subscription of such sums of money as each of us respectively
"promise and oblige ourselves to pay to Mr. Samuel Seabury
"aforesaid, yearly, in half-yearly payments, for the space of
"three years, for officiating amongst us : which subscription,
"we beg the Honourable Society to believe, will be punctually
"paid by the Honourable Society's most humble petitioners,
"the subscribers.

"H. LLOYD,

and others."

(From Ch. Doc. Conn. Hawks and Perry. p. 247, and quoted by the
late Rev. Dr. Moore in the History of St. George's Church, Hempstead.)

A. D. 1749.   Eight children baptized at Huntington, and
one adult, Elizabeth Bunt, at Hempstead. (Vide entries, &c.)

Here is inserted the original subscription list for the erection of a church building, with its date and preamble, as given
in an item which was probably copied from a paper on the History of Huntington Township written by the late Hon. Chas.
R. Street :—

" County of Suffolk, September, 1749.

" WHEREAS, There are a considerable number of persons in
" and about the town of Huntington of the Church of England,
" and there being no convenient house to meet in, we the sub-
" scribers do promise and agree to pay the respective sums to
" our names annexed, unto Henry Lloyd of the Manor of Queens
" Village, on or before the 1st day of May next after the date
" hereof, to be used in erecting a decent and convenient house
" for the worship of Almighty God according to the Liturgy of
" the Church of England as by law established, on some con-
" venient spot in the town of Huntington, which money so to
" be raised and paid to the aforesaid Henry Lloyd or order,
" shall be drawn out of his hands by a committee hereafter to
" be chosen by the major part of the subsribers for the carrying
" of ye building aforesaid. "

The following amounts were subscribed and duly paid by
the persons named :—

" Timothy Tredwell, £20 ; Dennis Wright, £3,9 ; Hannah
" Tredwell, £4 ; Isaiah Rogers, £20 ; Epenetus Platt, £5 ; Wil-
" liam Nicoll, Jr., £5 ; Richard Floyd, £3 ; Samuel De Honcur,
" £1 ; Monsieur Viele, £10 ; George Weiser, £5 ; Jos. Scid-
" more, £10 ; John Slaterly, £1 ; Isaac Brush, £20 ; Thomas
" Nethaway, £6 ; Monson Goold, £1 ; John Davis, £5 ; Wm.
" Mott, £3 ; Thos. Jarvis, £5 ; Samuel Ackerly, £5 ; John Ben-
" nett, £3 ; Benjamin Treadwell, £3 ; Eliphalet Smith, £3 ;
" given by Mr. Tredwell and others towards raising, £1,11 ;
" Total £140,1. The contribution of Henry Lloyd may be es-
" timated at £145."

Afterwards a supplementary subscription of £10 was raised
for glass for the windows which was brought from Boston.
(Item in a Parish paper published by Rev. A. Whitaker).

It appears from an item to be presently quoted that the land for the church building and for a burial ground was, in whole or in part, purchased in 1747.

An examination of the Lloyd letters (in possession of O. Egerton Schmidt, Esq.) has shown that as early as May 22, 1749, work on the church building was in progress. There are receipts, allowances on subscriptions, and a list of expenditures for such work, the latter aggregating £127,15,2 ; also a list of paid up subscriptions amounting to £140,1,0 ; also, *dated May 22, 1749*, a certificate of an auditing committee attesting these accounts. The writer concludes therefore that the date given at the head of the subscription list Sept'r 1749 " is a copyist's error, and should be "Sept'r 1747."

Undoubtedly the work begun in 1747, or early in 1748, was completed sometime in 1750. And the following receipt, an interesting document in itself as relating to the early labors of the first Bishop of the American Church, also gives evidence that in 1750, service was rendered " in the church."

" Received of Henry Lloyd Thirty Shillings which is in " full of his three first half-year's of his subscription for my ser- " vice in the church at Huntington, Nov'r 30th, 1750.
"SAM'L. SEABURY, JR."

A. D. 1750. May 12th. Two infants baptized by the Rev. Sam'l Seabury. (See entries &c.)

Oct. 5th. Mr. Seabury writes to the Society :—

" The Church at Huntington is also rendered very com- " modious, and a congregation of fifty or sixty persons, and " sometimes more, constantly attend Divine service there, who

"behave very devoutly and perform their part in Divine wor-
"ship very decently. They had taken from them in the late
"mortal sickness four of their most substantial members, who
"bore the principal part of building the church, which has
"very much weakened their ability, and they have desired me
"to ask of the Society a folio Bible and Common Prayer Book,
"for the use of the church."

A. D. 1751. Two baptisms (see entries &c.) Also Aug. 11th, marriage of Jehiel Seymore and Rachel Wright. Also, Nov. 17th, marriage "by license" of Isaac Rogers and Elizabeth Davis.

A. D. 1752. Marriage of Isaac Townsend and Hannah Youngs, (of Oyster Bay.)

"In July 1752, Mr. Seabury went to Edinburgh to study "Physic. He was ultimately Bishop of Connecticut." (Note in Parish Register.)

Oct'r 13th. Mr. Seabury writes to the S. P. G.

"My son laid down his place as Catechist at Huntington "in July last, and embarked from New York for Edinburgh in "August, to spend one year in studying of physic and anato- "my. The church has gained ground in Huntington by his "assistance, and under a discreet minister it would be a flour- "ishing church, notwithstanding the loss by death of its best "members." (Extract from Scrap-book of Mr. Henry Onder-donk.)

A. D. 1753. Eight baptisms. (See entries &c.)

A. D. 1754. One baptism. (See entries &c.)

A. D. 1755. Four baptisms. (See entries &c.)

Feb. 21st. Mr. Seabury writes that the church in the province of New York is truly militant, being continually attacked on one side or the other; sometimes by the enemies of Revelation, at other times by the wild enthusiasts; but in the midst of them true religion gains ground, and his churches of Hempstead, Oyster Bay and Huntington are crowded in good weather.

" I attend a full church at Huntington twice a year, on Sun-
" days: and at Huntington south, which is sixteen or seventeen
" miles from any church or meeting-house except Quakers.
" I have preached sundry times on week-days, to a congregation
" of one hundred people, generally poor, who express great
" thankfulness." (Extract from the Scrap-book of Mr. Henry Onderdonk.)

A. D. 1756.   Eleven baptisms.   (See entries &c.)

A. D. 1757.   One baptism.   (See entries &c.)

A. D. 1758.   Five baptisms.   (See entries &c.)

A. D. 1759.   Two baptisms.   (See entries &c.)

A. D. 1760.   Six baptisms, four being at Oyster Bay,
" negro slaves " of Dr. Platt.   (See entries &c.)

" From comparison of several statements, it is probable that a
" new church edifice was erected in 1760." (Note No. 2. in Parish register.)   It does not appear by whom this note was written, nor has the present editor been able to trace or verify the statements referred to.

A. D. 1761.   The Rev. Mr. Seabury, the Society's Missionary at Hempstead, in his letter of Oct'r 21st, 1761, after reference to other places which he visits, writes as follows :—

"The church at Huntington, where he can attend but "seldom, is well filled, and the zealous members always lament "their want of a minister." (From annals of the church on Long Island in Rev. A. Whitaker's Parish Record, March, 1885.)

Feb'y 26. Three baptisms by the Rev. S. Seabury. (See entries &c.)

April 28th. Married "by license," Isaac Ketcham and Freelove Carr.

July 5th. Nine baptisms by the Rev. S. Seabury. (See entries &c.)

Nov'r 15th. Four baptisms by the Rev. S. Seabury. (See entries &c.)

A. D. 1762. Extract from a letter of Mr. Seabury, Sen'r, dated Sept'r 30th, 1762. and published in the Abstract of the Proceedings of the Society for the Propagation of the Gospel. (England.)

" Abstract printed with the Sermon of 1763."

" He has also preached two Sundays to the people of Hunt- "ington, whose application for a missionary he begs leave to "recommend. The people of Huntington, as appears by their " own petition, and letters from Dr. Johnson and others, have "already erected an edifice for the worship of God according to " the Liturgy of the Church of England, and purchased a valu- " able House and Glebe worth about £200, that currency: which "they are ready to make a conveyance of for the use of the "church of Huntington forever, hoping to have leave within a "year or two, to send over a candidate for Holy Orders." (Note No. 3 in Parish Register.)

The mention, in this letter of Mr. Seabury's, of the "House and Glebe" makes a note upon that subject appropriate here. The tradition in the parish is that the land was of considerable extent, that a house still standing on the south side of Shoemaker Lane (formerly named Mill Dam Lane) is the house, and that the Rev. Mr. Greaton, the first rector, lived in it. The writer has been informed that the Rt. Rev. Horatio Potter, the late Bishop of New York, learned when in England attending the first Lambeth Conference that a deed or paper referring to a House and Glebe at Huntington was in the library at Lambeth Palace, (or more probably at Fulham, the See House of the Bishops of London, *Ed.*) But the authority for this statement was not mentioned.

The loss of the property is generally accounted for by the alleged moribund condition of the parish during the Revolutionary war and for several decades subsequent : in fact for about fifty years.   In Prime's History of Long Island it is stated that from the time of the death of the Rev. Mr. Greaton in 1773, no regular services were maintained.   " Indeed for many years," the history reads, " the house was not opened, and was literally " the undisturbed possession of bats and owls.   It was repaired, " however, about 40 years ago" (*i. e.* about 1805) "and ser-" vice re-established, but with considerable irregularity."

Now the *substantial* accuracy of this and somewhat similar statements to be presently quoted is unquestioned : although the payment of £5,6,0 in 1807 "for fourteen years service in " keeping records, *sweeping church* &c." seems inconsistent with the assertion of a complete abandonment of the building to the bats and owls.   And, as will presently be shown, we know that all through a period of twenty years following close upon the close of the war, though there appears to have been but occasional services, yet year by year the few faithful parishioners met to elect wardens and vestrymen, and thus the corporate existence was maintained.

That that which had been so steadily cared for between 1789 and 1809 was allowed to lapse afterwards, when the church had been repaired, and when there were occasional services held by the missionaries of the Diocese of New York, is of course possible, but not probable: although, apparently, that consequent time (from 1809 to 1829) was the time of greatest weakness. If the *organization* then lapsed, as perhaps it did, that may account for the loss of the property, although there is no known record of any seizure or sale.

Since the foregoing note was written, I have obtained the following item from the Rev. A. Whitaker's " Parish Record " of Dec'r 1885 :—

" The ground upon which the present church at Hunting-
" ton stands was purchased from Capt'n John Davis in 1747
" for £5. A few years later, this lot being found too small,
" measures were taken to enlarge the premises, and accord-
" ingly a committee purchased surrounding land to the extent
" of five acres. This committee, composed of Isaiah Rogers,
" Zopher Rogers, Jeremiah Rogers, Thomas Jarvis, Dr. Sam-
" uel Allen, and John Bennett, held the property at first as
" trustees. Fearing alienation, however, they conveyed the
" property in trust to the Society for the Propagation of the
" Gospel, to be held for the use of the Church of England.

" The land conveyed is described as five acres, bounded on
" the north by the highway leading over the Mill Dam, west
" by land of Timothy Kelsey, south by Israel Wood, and east

"by land laid out for the churchyard and the land of
"Capt'n Davis, deceased. This parcel seems to have
"extended north of the present church ground to Mill
"Dam lane. The glebe had upon it a house which was used
"afterwards as a rectory, and is stated in a letter by Mr. Sea-
"bury to have been worth £200. The land as early as 1680
"had been owned by Joseph Wood, and was afterwards sold by
"him to Thomas Jarvis. It stood in Mill Dam Lane " (*i. e.*
I suppose, the house so stood.) "Thomas Jarvis, it is
"thought, either donated or sold this property to the church."

"In 1770 the deeds of the glebe were annulled, and the
"title vested in the church-wardens for the use of the society,
"but the precise way in which it was done is not clear. After
"the death of the Rev. James Greaton, the first resident minis-
"ter of the Episcopal church in Huntington, his widow contin-
"ued to occupy the rectory on the glebe lands. She married
"Dr. B. Y. Prime in 1775, and lived for thirty years thereafter.
"Mr. Greaton had no successor in the vacant rectorship until
"1805, when for a short time the Rev. John C. Rudd took
"charge. Only a small part of the ancient glebe remains
"to-day, the rest having been alienated, but how and by whom
"is a question."

A. D. 1763. Jan'y 23d. Two baptisms. (For names &c.,
see entries &c.)

April 10th. Three baptisms. (See entries &c.) One of
these baptisms is thus recorded :—"Boston," negro male child
"of estate of H. Lloyd."

Sep't. "Four infants."

"In 1763, Mr. Kneeland was appointed reader to the
" church at Huntington by the Society. Mr. K. was then Cat-
" echist at Flushing." (Note No. 4 in Parish Register.)

He went to England for Holy orders in 1764, but apparently, judging from a letter written to Mr. Lloyd in 1765, did
not return to Huntington.

A. D. 1764. Three baptisms. (For names &c., see entries &c.)

" Rev. Samuel Seabury departed this life, Friday morning
" the 15th June, 1764, in the 58th year of his age, and is bur-
" ied at Hempstead. The next in order at Hempstead are rec-
" ords of Rev. Samuel Seabury (his son) who was at the time
"at Jamaica." (Note by Rev. Chas. H. Hall, D. D.)

" Between 1764 and 1766, the Rev. Sam'l Seabury, after-
" wards first Bishop of the country, and in those years settled
" at Grace church, Jamaica, occasionally ministered at Hunt-
" ington." (Note by the late Mr. Henry Lloyd.)

The deed conveying the five acres of land before referred
to the Society for the Propagation of the Gospel was executed
Aug. 21st of this year, It contains a " proviso " that Mr. Ebenezer Kneeland be admitted to Holy orders to serve as Rector or
Missionary at Huntington.

Feb. 17th. In Huntington, which Dr. Johnson recommends for a mission, there are about forty families, and if Oyster Bay was annexed, thirty or forty more : but on the south
side of Long Island, to which they extend, there are not less
than one hundred who have no teacher of any sort. (Extract
from the Scrap-book of Mr. Henry Onderdonk.)

A. D. 1765. Feb. 10th. A salary of £10 allowed to Mr. E. Kneeland, catechist at Huntington.

A. D. 1767. "In 1767, the Rev. Mr." (James) "Greaton was settled as Rector at Huntington : died in 1773." (Note No. 5 in Parish Register.)

The Rev. Leanord Cutting, settled at Hempstead from 1766—1784, visited Huntington as follows, for the office of baptism, &c." (Note by Rev. C. H. Hall, D. D.)

Here follow the records of thirty baptisms by Rev. L. Cutting, viz.: four in 1767, two in 1768, one in 1772, one in 1773, and the others in the years following, as hereafter given.

A. D. 1768. Nov. 30th. The church wardens and vestry of Huntington lay before the venerable society " their unhappy circumstances." In Huntington, and Queen's village, five miles distant, are upwards of thirty heads of families, professors of the church of England, who are destitute of the administration of God's word and Sacraments. Mr. Kneeland was employed to read prayers and sermons, and subsequently sent to England for Orders. Henry Lloyd of Boston recommends Mr. Greaton of Boston, at a salary of £20, with firewood, a house, and glebe. His services to include Islip and Queens village. (Extract from the scrap-book of Mr. Henry Onderdonk).

The statement, then, in Note No. 5 in the Parish register, that Mr. Greaton was " settled as Rector in 1767 " is incorrect. He began work in 1769, and received appointment as one of the Society's missionaries in 1770, with an allowance of £40. The information as to date of missionary appointment and amount of allowance is from Mr. Henry Onderdonk's Scrap-book. (Editor).

A. D. 1769 August 8th. Mr. Greaton, at Boston, (on a visit) writes :

" At Huntington I have a very decent congregation who
" almost constantly attend. Frequently a number of dissenters
" come to hear me, who behave with the utmost decency, and
" seem much pleased. Several times I have had the church so
" full that it could not conveniently hold more, and many were
" obliged to go away for want of room. I flatter myself that in
" time a flourishing church may be raised up there, if the peo-
" ple are so happy as to continue to enjoy the smiles of the So-
" ciety. The people have purchased a new glebe, with a good
" house, at a cost of £344, currency, which they propose to
" make over to the society in lieu of the old glebe, which cost
" only £120." (Extract from scrap-book of Mr. Henry Onder-
" donk).

The records and notes preceding had all been written or compiled before the important statement in Mr. Greaton's letter concerning the purchase of a " *new* glebe and house " came to notice.

Nothing is said as to the *location* of the new house and glebe : and I may cite in this connection a statement made to me by an esteemed former parishioner and vestryman, whose time of residence in Huntington covered many years, that he had the impression, from tradition derived, he thought, from descendants of Mr. Greaton, that the house in which Mr. Greaton died, and from which his body was brought for interment, was not near the church, but down in the valley near the present village, on what is called Spring street.

However this may be, there are expressions in a letter written in 1780, and given hereafter in full under that date, which show that what was *then* the parsonage was, with its grounds, near the church. "The parsonage house," the writer states, "is in tolerable repair, but the barn has suffered in common with the church; *i. e.* from their use, or rather abuse, by the British troops; having been "taken for barracks."

We have to conclude, then, either that the purchase of the new house and glebe was not finally consummated, or else that that house and glebe was, like the old one, near the church. And it is evident from the value stated that the house was a better one, and the glebe of larger extent, than those obtained by the original purchase, which according to Mr. Greaton, was effected for £120, although valued by Mr. Seabury at £200.

In the year following (A. D. 1770) Mr. Henry Lloyd sent from Boston to Joseph Lloyd at Queen's village deeds for this new house and glebe, (see appendix on deeds &c., relating to the glebe) executed to the church wardens, with a request that the wardens execute a deed (also enclosed) "to the society;" *i. e.* to the S. P. G. This letter has evidently been a puzzle to the writers of precedent notes on the glebe, but when read in connection with Mr. Greaton's letter, above given, its wording and purpose become clear.

Much, however, as to the details and consummation of this purchase, and the subsequent loss or alienation of all the property except the narrow strip on which the old church stood, remains uncertain. All that we know is this,—that the parish possessed, and had in use, either the old or the new house and glebe, as late as the year 1780, and probably at the close of the war : that in 1787, two deeds of "the old glebe" were sent back from London by Mr. H. Lloyd, and that at that time and for at least twenty years afterwards, the corporate existence of the parish was maintained.

A. D. 1770. "This same year Mr. James Greaton is ap-"pointed Missionary at Huntington with an allowance of £40, "having been licensed January 28, 1760, by the Bishop of Lon-"don." (From History of St. George's, Hempstead, by the "late Rev. Dr. Moore.)

A. D. 1773. The Rev. Jas. Greaton, first settled Rector, departed this life.

Jan. 13th. Mr. Greaton's account of his mission at Hunt-ington was a very acceptable one to the society. They lament his death, which, has since happened, and the circumstances of his family, which have been represented to them as necessitous.

April 17th. Died, at Huntington, after a short illness (said to have been attended with fits,) the Rev. James Greaton, Episcopal minister at that place, and formerly of Christ Church, Boston. (Extract from the Scrap-book of Mr Henry Onderdonk.)

A. D. 1774. Dec. 29th. Two baptisms by the Rev. L. Cutting. (For names &c., see entries &c.)

Dec. 29th. "Admitted into " the church " * James and
Mary Greaton, Richard, son of Obadiah Hammond, slave of
Mr. Loyd, Rachel, slave of Dr. Platt.

Dec. 29th. Last Sunday sennit, at Huntington, B. Y.
Prime, M. D. was married to the amiable Mrs. Mary (Wheel-
wright), relict of the Rev. James Greaton. (Extract from the
scrap-book of Mr. Henry Onderdonk.)

A. D. 1775. June 15th. Five baptisms by Rev. L. Cutting. (See entries &c.)

" Under date of Feb. 17th, 1775, Mr. Cutting mentions
" that a petition had been received from the church wardens
" &c. in Huntington, Brookhaven, Islip and Queen's Village "
(Lloyd's Neck) " for a missionary in the place of their late
" worthy pastor, Mr. Greaton, with the former allowance from
" the Society, to which they hope they shall be able to add £20.
" But the Society, considering the proposed subscription as in-
" sufficient, nor properly engaged for, on the part of the peti-
" tioners, have thought it advisable for the present to postpone
" the application." (From Dr. Moore's History of St. George's,
Hempstead.)

A. D. 1777. Six baptisms by Rev. L. Cutting. (See entries &c.)

" I have not attended the vacant church at Huntington
" this last year, as the principal persons of my congregation
" thought it by no means advisable for me to go out of my own

---

" * Probably James, son of Mary Greaton, widow of Rev. J. Greaton." Note by Rev. C. B. Ellsworth.)

"parish." (Extract from letter of Rev. L. Cutting to S. P. G. Jan'y 6th, 1777.)

A. D. 1779. Nov'r 26. Rev. Chas. Inglis writes from New York, (to the S. P. G.)

" The only vacant mission on Long Island is that at Hunt-
" ington, but no loyal clergyman dare settle there ; that part of
" the island is infested by Rebels who are constantly making
" excursions across the Sound, plundering the inhabitants, and
" carrying many of them off captives." (Extract from Scrap-
book of Mr. Henry Onderdonk.)

A. D. 1730. Eleven baptisms by Rev. L. Cutting. (See entries &c.)

May 18th. Rev. Mr. Waller writes from New York, (to the S. P. G.)

" I was last Sunday at Huntington, and officiated for the
" first time this season at that church, to a small but attentive
" congregation. The church which till last winter had remained
" untouched amid the desolations of war, was then taken by
" the (British) army for barracks, and according to custom,
" greatly abused and damaged. The parsonage house is in tol-
" erable repair, but the barn has suffered in common with the
" church. Several of the principal families have gone into the
" rebellion, but their places are supplied by a number of refu-
" gees from Connecticut, who, uniting with the remaining fam-
" ilies, are desirous, notwithstanding their discouragements, to
" keep the service among them. I have promised to visit them
" once a month till winter, and I hope to prevail on some of

"our refugee clergy here to do the same." (Extract from scrap-book of Mr. Henry Onderdonk.)

A. D. **1782**. Twelve baptisms by Rev. L. Cutting. (See entries &c.)

A. D. **1783**. One baptism &c. After this date until 1838, a period of fifty-five years, we know of but *one* baptism, viz.: by the Rev. Seth Hart, of Hempstead, in 1804.

Also, in 1783, married, "per license," Adam Lefferts, of Oyster Bay and Rebecca Conklin of Huntington.

"Year of Peace and end of Colonial times. This year Rev. L. Cutting "removed to the South." (Note by Dr. Hall.)

"Rev. —— Rowland, father of N. S. Rowland of New "York, accepted the care (of the parish) during the Revolution-"ary war, but as his household goods and library were captured "by the British on their way out, he soon became discouraged, "and went to Nova Scotia." (Note in a list Mss. of Rectors compiled by Mr. Oscar Egerton Schmidt.)

"During the Revolution, occasional services were held at "Huntington, *e. g.* in 1780 by the Revs. Wm. Waller and "John Sayre, and also by the chaplains belonging to English "forces who were from time to time stationed there .... In "1782, the Rev. T. L. Moore, afterwards rector at Hempstead, "officiated at Huntington, Setauket and Islip ; as did also the "Rev. Andrew Fowler in 1789. From that time on until 1806 "the priestly functions were generally suspended throughout "the county." (*i. e.* of Suffolk.) "An occasional service may "have been held, but it must have been exceptional." (Note in Rev. A. Whitaker's Parish Record, Feb. 1886.)

"The Rector or Incumbent seven years before the Revo-"lutionary war is buried under the Altar." (Extract from a letter from the Rev. N. Barrows.) The reference is to the body of the Rev. James Greaton, of whom also the large east window is in memory.

A. D. 1788. March 1st. The earliest *original* record in our possession begins with this date. This, and following records, dated 1789 and 1790, and also two brief entries dated 1797 and 1800, are on two discolored sheets of paper, letter size, stitched together but unbound, forming eight pages ; the greater part of the half sheet which makes the first and second pages being torn away. The said records relate chiefly to meetings of "the Episcopal congregation" for election of wardens and vestrymen, (the latter, like the former, being but two in number,) held on March 1st in each year. In 1788 a *vestry meeting* was held, and another in 1790. Resolutions passed at the former are sub-joined, as a matter of curious interest.

"*Resolved*, That the church Be Repaired so far as to Shingal the south side of the Ruff & seet the Body and glaze it."

"*Resolved*, That John Johnson be appointed to get the meterals and oversee the Bisiness."

"*Resolved*, That all Parsons that have any Wrights In the Pues that Do Not Repair the same Within Six Months from this date shall Bee as is forfeited to said church."

JOHN JONES,   } *Wardens*
ADAM LEFFORD,   }

JOHN JOHNSON,   } *Vestry*
ISAAC YOUNGS,   }

In 1788, the parish was represented in the convention of the diocese of New York by Isaac Youngs, who joined with the representatives of Brookhaven and Oyster Bay in asking that Mr. Andrew Fowler be recommended to the Bishop for Holy Orders.

In 1789, Nov. 5th. " Rev. Mr. Fowler, of Huntington, "appeared, and took his seat in convention." In 1790, Mr. Fowler is noted as " Rector of Christ church, Oyster Bay." In 1806, St. John's church, Huntington, was represented by Shubael Smith.

A. D. 1793. On March 21st, this year, and on the same date in each following year to 1805, inclusive, a meeting was held for the election of wardens and vestrymen. Brief records of these meetings, also certain church accounts for the same time, are entered in a long narrow book which had been partly used as the "Account Book" of a Military Company in the Revolutionary Army, and for which the vestry in 1801 paid to Shubael Smith "by agreement of the wardens" the sum of eight shillings. The original minutes of Vestry meetings from 1838 to 1856 were also written in the same book.

A. D. 1804. July 29th. One baptism by Rev. Seth Hart. "David Smith Conklin, son of Elkanah and Rebecca Conklin." (Extract from Register of St. George's, Hempstead.)

A. D. 1806. " In this year, the Rev. J. C. Rudd was "sent as Missionary into Suffolk County by the Bishop of New

" York.   He succeeded in stirring up anew the interest of the
" few remaining Churchmen, but it was only for a short time.
" He withdrew to more inviting fields."   (Note in Rev. A.
" Whitaker's Parish Record, Feb. 1886.)

The following is an extract from the Missionary Report,
printed in the Journal of the N. Y. Convention :—

" In Huntington, Mr. Rudd found it difficult for some time
" to rouse the dormant zeal for the church of the few scattered
" families who still professed themselves its members.   By the
" blessing of God upon his labors, he at length happily suc-
" ceeded.   The ministration of the excellent worship of the
" church revived the former attachment of its former members to
" it : and before Mr. Rudd left them, they made arrangements
" for repairing their place of public worship, which was in a
" very decayed state.   The Committee are happy to be assured
" that the zeal which has been excited still continues, and that
" the congregation look forward with earnest hope to the time
" when the blessing of God upon their exertions will enable
" them to restore the church among them in " the beauty
" of holiness."

A. D. 1807.   About $100 were subscribed and paid for a
new roof and plastering walls.   Another item mentions the
payment to Mr. ——— of £5,16,0, for fourteen years' service in
keeping records, sweeping church, &c.

A. D. 1809.   April 8th.   " Rev. Feltis " (probably the
Rev. H. J. Feltus, rector of St. Ann's Brooklyn, from 1807 to
1814) " administered the Sacrament : there were five commu
" nicants : a young gentleman, Elkanah Conklin, Abby Hew-

" lett, Shubael Smith, Freelove Smith." (Note in Parish Register.)

A. D. 1814. " Rev. Chas. Seabury, of Setauket, offici-
" ated twelve times." (Note in Parish Register.)

He probably visited Huntington at intervals from 1814 to
1827.

" Rev. Chas. Seabury, son of the Bishop, was appointed
" to care of Setauket, with charge also of Huntington and
" Islip." (Note in Rev. A. Whitaker's " Parish Record ".)

A. D. 1823. " The last Sunday in September, Rev. Ed-
" ward K. Fowler took charge of the parish, in which no reg-
" ular service but the above" (*i. e.* those mentioned under dates
preceding,) " was held for sixteen years. He remained until
" towards the close of 1826." (Note in Parish Register.)

What the writer of the foregoing note means by " regular
service " is not clear : for even those services to which he refers as exceptions to his main statement were themselves but
occasional : *i. e.* they were not continuous or periodical. He
probably means, however, that during the sixteen years, none
but occasional services had been held. In fact, with the possible
exception of those incidental to the brief ministry of Dr. Rudd
in 1805 or 1806, none other services had been held for *fifty*
years. For exactly that number of years had passed between
the death of Mr. Greaton in 1773 and the settlement of Mr.
Fowler in 1823. But all through this long time, apparently,
at intervals of but a few years at most, there *were* such services,
some of them held possibly elsewhere, but most of them doubtless in the church. And for a number of years,—probably in

those preceding the war, (during which years, as appears from the Lloyd letters, attempts were being made to secure a successor to Mr. Greaton,) and certainly from 1788 to 1807, at least,—the parochial organization seems to have been carefully maintained. From 1807 to 1837, elections of parish officers may possibly have ceased : and it is evident that the work became dependent, during that period, upon such missionary effort as could be put forth by the diocese of New York.

No records of the official acts of the first rector, Rev. James Greaton, (1769 to 1773) or of the Rev. Ed. K. Fowler, (1823 to 1826) have as yet been found. The latter is referred to in the Convention Journals of the diocese of New York as " Deacon, " and Missionary at Huntington."

A. D. 1826.   From Nov. 1826 to April 1827, the Rev. Samuel Seabury was in charge. He was a son of the Rev. Chas. Seabury, of Setauket, and at this time was in Deacon's Orders, serving as Missionary at Huntington under the Missionary Committee of the diocese of New York. He was transferred to work at Hailett's Cove in 1827, was afterwards Editor of " The Churchman," N. Y., Rector of the Church of the Annunciation, N. Y., and finally Professor of Biblical Learning in the Gen. Theo. Seminary.

A. D. 1827.   The Rev. Chas. Seabury reports visiting Huntington in the Spring, and administering Holy Communion, his son being in Deacon's Orders.

A. D. 1834.   It is stated in one of the notes in " Annals of Suffolk Co." in the Rev. A. Whitaker's " Parish Record " that the Rev. Isaac Sherwood was this year appointed to the charge of St. John's Huntington.

Mr. Sherwood also had charge of St. John's, Cold Spring, resided there, and probably served this parish for some years as missionary. But in the record of the Act of Incorporation (1838) which follows, he is styled "Rector."

A. D. 1838. The original records of Vestry elections and meetings, which were not carried beyond 1809, are resumed this year, and the first record is that of the Incorporation of the Parish. This was effected on May 7th, the names of the then Rector, Wardens and Vestrymen being as follows :—

Rector,   REV. ISAAC SHERWOOD.
Wardens,   DAN'L W. KISSAM,
          JOHN R. RHINELANDER.
Vestrymen,   ABRAHAM VAN WYCK,
          WILLIAM C. STOUT,
          NATH. BLOODGOOD,
          WILL'M M. HAWTHORNE.
          JOEL PLATT,
          CHAS. P. STEWART,
          HIRAM PAULDING,
          WILLIAM HEWLETT.

A. D. 1843. On June 9th, a resolution relinquishing the aid of the Missionary Committee was adopted; and a few weeks afterwards the Rev. J. Sherwood resigned, and was succeeded by the Rev. Moses Marcus.

Twenty baptisms by the Rev. J. Sherwood are recorded.

A. D. 1844. On Oct. 22d., the Rev. Moses Marcus resigned the rectorship.

In a long note in pencil in the record book, Mr. Marcus gives an account of the services maintained by him, and of the disposition of offertories, noting the Rector's right to dispense what has been offered as "alms and oblations at the Sacrament of the Lord's Supper." He also states that in addition to the services at the Church, he has held a third service every Lord's day evening in the District School Room on East Neck ; that these services have been well attended, and that "the little flock gives promise of usefulness and increase to the church."

Mr. Marcus was evidently a faithful and earnest priest, but also a rigidly conservative and perhaps somewhat militant churchman of the old school. In the concluding paragraph of his note he thus frees his mind :—

"The church is probably the oldest in the diocese." (This is an error ; at the time of writing there were several older, and one of them, at Setauket in this county, is still standing, and in use. Ed.) "It was built by the Society for the Propagation "of the Gospel, and has had among its ministers the Rt. Rev. "Bishop Seabury, the Rev. Chas. Seabury and the Rev. Sam'l "Seabury, D. D., also Bishops Hobart and Onderdonk, the "Rev. Dr. Rudd, Rev. Ed. K. Fowler, &c., &c."

"As a relick of the olden time, its general character should "have been preserved, and its venerable pulpit never removed "from its place : but this is the age of innovation, and so old "things have passed away, and all things are to become new ! "But, as Bishop Brownell, when here last year, very properly "observed, the old church ought to be kept entire, and a new "Church built in the Village (proper) of Huntington, where it

"is needed, and where the Church would at once increase.
"On the other hand, it is to be feared that the spirit of exclu-
"siveness, which unhappily prevails throughout the parish,
"will prevent any extraordinary increase where the Church
"now is, let the Vestry do what they may. The rich and the
"poor are equal in God's sight, and ought so to be treated by
"all Christian men : but they have not been, and hence there
"is the greatest prejudice against the Church among the inhab-
"itants generally."

Whatever may be thought as to the strictures and opinions
expressed by Mr. Marcus, it is much to be regretted that the
sage advice of Bishop Brownell was not regarded when, sometime after, the question of a new church was under considera-
tion. The old church should indeed have been preserved "as
a relick of the olden time," and the new church built nearer
the Village. From an æsthetic point of view the present building and its surroundings are admirable ; but its distance from
the Village and its single roundabout and "up hill and down
dale" approach are serious weights upon the growth and avail
ability of the work.

As many as twenty baptisms by Mr. Marcus during his
short rectorship are recorded.

A. D. 1845. On April 1st, the Rev. Chas. H. Hall be
came rector, being at the time in Deacon's Orders, but was or
dained to the Priesthood the same year. He administered
twenty-five baptisms, prepared six candidates for Confirmation,
and officiated at seven burials.

By a happy coincidence, this same year (1895) will
mark fifty years from the Rev. Dr. Hall's Ordination to the

Priesthood, and one hundred and fifty from the date of the organization of the Parish, or the beginning of definite work in this place. It is hoped that suitable arrangement may be made for the celebration of the conjoint anniversary.

A. D. 1847. On June 2d, the Rev. C. Donald McLeod became rector, being, like his predecessor, in Deacon's Orders, and also being similarly advanced to the Priesthood during his rectorship. He officiated at six baptisms, one marriage and three burials.

A. D. 1848. The Rev. C. D. McLeod resigned the rectorship.

From this year to 1853, there are no minutes of the Vestry. From the records, however, in the Parish Register it appears that the Rev. F. W. Shelton became rector in 1848, one baptism by him being recorded, and three marriages, one in each of the years 1848, 1849, and 1850. He also presented three candidates for Confirmation, the sacred Rite being administered by the Rt. Rev. Bishop Chase.

A. D. 1852. One baptism by the " Rev. Mr. Seymour " is recorded, and one by the Rev. A. Guion.

In August of this year the Rev. W. A. W. Maybin became rector.

A. D. 1853. Sept. 15th. John R. Rhinelander, one of the Wardens since 1838, resigned that office. He was subsequently in one year (1856) elected a Vestryman, but apparently did not serve.

A. D. 1856. July 26th. Rev. W. A. W. Maybin resigned the rectorship, accepting a call to St. Paul's Church, Williamsburgh.

Oct. The Rev. Wm. G. Farrington became rector, with a salary of $400 per annum.

A. D. 1858. July 4th. Rev. W. G. Farrington resigned.

Aug. The Rev. James H. Williams became rector, with a salary of $450 per annum.

A. D. 1859. July 14. The resignation of the Rector, offered in January in consequence of ill health, was at this time accepted with expressions of great regret.

Sept. 12th. Rev. Wm. J. Lynd, having been secured as rector for one year, was introduced to the Vestry, receiving the keys of the Church from the Senior Warden. Salary $500 per annum.

A. D. 1860. At a meeting of the Vestry, held April 12th, it was "resolved, that this Vestry do now take the neces-"sary steps to build a new church."

At a meeting held May 18th it was "resolved, that the "Vestry now express their feelings in regard to a change of "site by voting upon the following :—

"*Resolved*, That when we build a new church we will "build it upon a new site. Ayes, Ray, Adams, Scudder, "Williams, Fleet, Atwater, Nicoll, 7. Nays, William C. "Stout, 1."

At a subsequent meeting, on Aug. 2nd, a resolution was passed rescinding the foregoing.

At this meeting on Aug. 2nd, it was also "resolved, that " the thanks of the Vestry be rendered to Rev. Mr. Lynd for " his researches into the old time history of St. John's Church " in Huntington, and for the interesting facts presented by him " relative thereto."

No record, however, of the facts presented seems to have come to us, except, possibly some of the Notes in the Parish Register.

Aug. 14th, the Rev. W. J. Lynd, though requested to remain as rector until Easter 1862, decided to "accept a call in the City " of New York."

At a meeting on this date, it was "resolved, that a new " church be built on the old site."

No record appears of the call or induction of the Rev. Caleb B. Ellsworth, but he probably entered upon his charge about the close of the year. A list of rectors &c., compiled by Mr. O. E. Schmidt, gives the date Nov. 1860. The salary was fixed, at a meeting in Feb. 1861, at $600.

A. D. 1861. Sept. 7th. The "Committee to procure " additional land for the church " reported that they had "pur- " chased from Mrs. Bunce a strip of land of 15 feet front and " 419 feet in depth, adjoining the church lands and on the " south side of the same, for the sum of $225; and that the " Deed for said strip of land was in the possession of the Clerk " of the Vestry."

The "Committee to procure subscriptions and build a new " church " reported that "the Committee had closed a contract

" with Edwin Wood & Co., for four thousand seven hundred
" and fifty dollars ($4,750) including all mason work, with in-
" side and outside carpenter work, and outside painting ; and
" that the inside painting and decoration would probably
" cost the additional sum of $250."

A. D. 1862. April 30th. At a Vestry meeting held on
this date, on motion of Richard B. Post, it was " resolved, that
" in view of the proposed Consecration of this Church on the
" 6th of May next, the Rector and the Clerk of the Vestry be
" authorized to prepare and to sign in behalf of the Vestry the
" proper Instrument of Donation."

Also, on motion of Joseph H. Ray, it was " resolved, that
" this Vestry fully appreciate the indefatigable services of
" Mr. Hewlett Long, as devoted to the procurement of a bell
" for the Church, and to the advancement of the general inter-
" ests of the Parish : and hereby tenders him its grateful thanks."

The thanks of the Vestry were also presented to Mr. Gilbert P. Williams " for his faithful discharge during many years
" of the duties of Collector," and also to Mrs. Philipse " for her
" beautiful donation of a silver Communion Service to our
" Church."

Sunday, May 4th. At a meeting of the Congregation held
after morning service, resolutions of respect and esteem, with
suitable preamble, relative to the death of the Hon. C. C. Cam-
brelling, were unanimously adopted.

May 6th. " The new church of the ancient parish of St.
" John's, Huntington, L. I., was consecrated by the Bishop of
" the Diocese on Tuesday, May 6th, twelve of the clergy being

" present in surplices, and taking part in the interesting ser-
" vices of the day. The Bishop and Clergy moved in proces-
" sion to the porch under the tower, where they were met by
" the Wardens and Vestrymen, and entered the Church saying
" alternately the twenty-fourth Psalm. The Senior Warden
" having handed the Bishop the Instrument of Donation and
" Request, it was read by the Rev. Mr. Williams, of Smithtown.
" The Sentence of Consecration was read by the Rev. Mr. Hut-
" ton, of Oyster Bay. Morning Prayer was begun by the Rev.
" Wm. G. Farrington of New York, the Lessons being read by
" the Rev. Mr. Moore of Hempstead and the Rev. Mr. Statham
" of Patchogue, and the Creed and Prayers said by the Rev. J.
" H. Williams of Dobb's Ferry. The Bishop began the Ante-
" Communion Service, the Epistle being read by the Rev. Mr.
" Edwards, and the Gospel by the Rev. E. K. Fowler, who
" had ministered in the parish more than forty years before.
" The Sermon was preached by the Rev. Dr. Seabury of New
" York, from the text, " Put off thy shoes from off thy feet,
" for the place whereon thou standest is Holy Ground." The
" *relative* holiness of the House of God, and the duty of rever-
" encing the sanctuary, were forcibly set forth.

" After the Sermon, the Bishop proceeded with the rite of
" Confirmation, the preface being read by the Rector, the Rev.
" C. B. Ellsworth, and sixteen persons received the laying-on
" of hands. In his address to the newly-confirmed, the Bishop,
" after alluding to the beauty of the new temple, and the im-
" pressive services in which they had just been engaged,
" brought out very happily the analogies between the consecra-
" tion of the material temple to the worship and service of the
" Almighty, and the solemn offering and consecration of the

"living temple as 'a reasonable, holy,' and living sacrifice
"unto God."

"The Offertory Sentences were read by the Rev. Mr. Mal-
"laby, and the Exhortation and following parts of the Commu-
"nion Office by the Rev. Dr. Porter. The Bishop said the
"Prayer of Consecration, and administered to the clergy and a
"very large number of the laity. Despite the great length of
"the service, the entire congregation, though composed in
"great part of those not of the Church, remained to the very
"end, evidently deeply impressed by what they had seen and
"heard, and seemingly loth to depart from the Gate of Heaven."

In another paragraph of this communication the statement
appears that the old church had been " repaired and renovated
" in the year 1838, and a Vestry having been organized, it was
" consecrated by Bishop Onderdonk."

"The designs for the new church were furnished by Gage
"Inslee, of New York. The stained glass was made by Dore-
"mus, and the decorating was done by Otto Ficht."

"Four of the clergymen who took part in the service had
"been ministers of the parish, viz.: the Rev. Dr. Seabury and
"the Rev. Messrs. Fowler, Farrington and J. H. Williams."
(From "Correspondence of the Church Journal.")

A. D. 1855. April 17th. At the Parish Meeting on this
day, Easter Monday, a preamble and resolutions, offered by
Mr. Wm. Nicoll, Senior Warden, appropriate to the national
distress occasioned by the assassination of President Lincoln,
was unanimously adopted, and it was ordered that the church
should be draped in mourning.

A. D. 1867. Feb. 3rd. The Convention of the Diocese of New York having called for an expression of opinion as to the erection of this part of the State into a new diocese, the following resolution, at a Vestry Meeting held on this date, was adopted :—

" *Resolved*, That in the judgment of this Vestry, the erec-" tion of a new diocese in the southern part of the diocese of " New York, to consist of Long Island, *is desirable*."

April 18th, At a Vestry Meeting held on this date, the Treasurer reported the receipt on Jan. 11th last of four hundred and eighty-four and 30-100 dollars as the proceeds of a bequest made to the Vestry of this Church by Mrs. John R. Rhinelander, deceased.

At the same meeting it was

" *Resolved*, That we regret the removal from our midst of " Mr. Wm. Nicoll, our Senior Warden ; and we tender him our " thanks for the interest he has manifested in the welfare of " our church during his sojourn here, and particularly for his " counsel and his invaluable services rendered in connection " with the building of our church edifice."

A most cordial response in a letter from Mr. Nicoll was read to a subsequent meeting, and will be found spread upon the Minutes, as was directed.

A. D. 1868. At a meeting of the Vestry, held Sept. 10th. The "Committee on Episcopate Fund" reported that they had raised and paid over to John D. Jones, Treasurer of the Long Island Episcopate Fund the sum of two hundred dollars, being the amount assessed on St. John's Church, Huntington.

At a subsequent meeting, on Nov. 14th, on motion of Chas.
H. Fleet, it was

"*Resolved*, That the following named persons be duly ap-
" pointed Lay Delegates to attend the Primary Diocesan Con-
" vention of the Protestant Episcopal Church on Long Island,
" to be held on Wednesday, Nov. 18th, at the Church of the
" Holy Trinity in the City of Brooklyn : viz.: Edward Kissam,
" Isaac Adams, and Hiram Paulding, Jr."

A. D. 1870.   Report to Convention this year shows eighty-
two Communicants and total offerings of $1,056.

At a meeting of the Vestry, held Oct. 22nd, the Rev. C.
B. Ellsworth, rector, tendered his resignation, which was accepted, with an expression of regret and good wishes.

Thus the rectorship became vacant, after being occupied
by Mr. Ellsworth for nearly ten years, the longest term as yet
reached by any rector of this parish.

The " Committee to procure a rector" seem to have met
with considerable difficulty, two " calls " being declined, and
several urgent appeals were made by the Committee for larger
means and increased interest.   And the great disadvantage of
having a church on a site which is inconvenient to a considerable number of people also begins to make itself manifest.   " It
requires some special attraction " say the Committee, " to draw
a congregation."   And they appeal for special means to meet
this disadvantage, " since," they add, " the church cannot be
moved to a more convenient location."

A. D. 1871. The Rev. Alfred J. Barrow accepted a call to the Rectorship of this parish, on May 1st, 1871, at a salary of $1,200 per annum.

Soon afterwards, the church was supplied with lamps for furnishing light for evening services at a cost to the parish of $140, two chandeliers with lamps being added at the cost of Mr. I. E. Doying, and a brick furnace was erected in the basement at a cost of about $200.

Also, in August of the same year, a fund of $1,400 having been obtained, largely through the efforts of the Ladies' Parish Aid Society, contract was made with Geo. W. Earle, Organ-builder, of Riverhead, for a new Pipe-Organ, for the sum of $1,750. The old organ was presented to "the Missionary Chapel at Riverhead."

A. D. 1872. March 28th. Treasurer reports "Total Re- "ceipts $1,573.33, Total Disbursements $1,566.39, Balance in "hand $6.94: also in hand L. I. Gillespie's note for $600 (Rhinelander Fund) bearing interest at 7 per cent "

Rector's Report to Convention shows "Confirmed, 15 : "Communicants, 90 : Contributions for Current Expenses, "$1,549 : Total Parochial Offerings, $5,137 ; Total Offering, "$5,242. Also the purchase of a new and beautiful organ for "$1,960. Also, an acre of land adjoining the Church property "for parsonage purposes and Horse-sheds for $1,000: mainly "due to the exertions of an active Society of ladies. Rector's "study furnished, new surplice given, &c., estimated at $100. "Improvement of Church property by lighting and heating "$350. Occasional services at Centreport and Northport."

A. D. 1873. New Carriage Road made, parallel with the old lot, grounds partially graded, and new fences put up, at a cost of $120. Also, thirteen Horse-Sheds erected, costing $566, this being contributed by those to whom sheds were assigned, with $50 from Mr. A. Mulligan.

Report to Convention showed Confirmations, 10 ; Communicants, 92 ; Current Expenses, $1,983 ; All Parochial, $3,953 ; All Contributions, $4,069.

A. D. 1874. Report to Convention showed Communicants, 103 ; Current Expenses, $1,884 ; Subscription to Rectory Fund, $2,150 ; Total Parochial, $4,216 ; Total Offerings, $4,511.

A. D. 1875. In March of this year the Rectory was completed, at a total cost of $5,115. Of this amount the " Ladies' Rectory Fund Society " had furnished the large sum of $2,451.51 : the Rhinelander Fund, which had grown to $685.26 was appropriated to this purpose, and there were other subscriptions amounting to $1,335. The balance, $643.55 and about $900 expended in furnishing were raised by a mortgage of $1,500 for three years upon the property.

Report to Convention showed Communicants, 117 ; Confirmed, 12 ; Current Expenses, $1,912 ; Total for Parochial Purposes, $2,833 ; Total Offerings $3,111.

A. D. 1876. A dispute concerning the election for Wardens and Vestrymen was referred to the Hon. Murray Hoffman, and was decided adversely to those who contested the Rector's decision.

Report to Convention showed Communicants, 115 ; Confirmed, 6 ; Current Expenses, $1,870 ; Total for Parochial Purposes, $3,021 ; Total Offerings, $3,263.

A. D. 1877. At a meeting of the Vestry held May 19th, the Rev. A. J. Barrow, having received a call to Brooklyn, tendered his resignation, which was accepted, and a Committee was appointed to draft resolutions of regret and esteem.

The Rev. Thaddeus A. Snively accepted election to the Rectorship, and took charge of the Parish on July 15th.

Report to Convention showed Communicants, 97 ; Confirmed, 3 ; Current Expenses, $1,526 ; Total Parochial, $2,012 ; Total Offerings, $2,157.

A. D. 1878. At a meeting of the Vestry held Feb. 16th, resolutions were passed expressive of the sense of the Church's loss in the death of Mr. Sam'l W. Jones, a valued and esteemed member of the Vestry.

Also, the resignation of the Rector, Rev. T. A. Snively, was accepted with much regret.

At a subsequent meeting, on April 13th, the vacant Rectorship was tendered to the Rev. N. Barrows, of Rahway, N. J. Mr. Barrows accepted, and took charge on May 1st.

Report to Convention showed (May 21st) Communicants, 105 ; Current Expenses, $1,444.33 ; All Parochial Expenses, $1,915.61 ; Total Offerings, $2,189.30. In June of this year, Mr. Wm. A. M. Diller, of Brooklyn, was engaged to instruct a Choir, and on Sunday, Aug. 25th, a vested choir, of eight men and fifteen boys, was introduced. The chancel was extended four feet into the nave ; desks and seats were provided at an expense of about $100. The pulpit was moved, and the font placed at the west end of the church. A Choir-room, 27 feet by 11 feet, was built at the north-west end of the church, chiefly through the liberality of Mr. Ira E. Doying.

A. D. 1879. Parochial Report (May 20th) showed Confirmed, 10 ; Communicants, 108 ; For Current Expenses, $1,509.66 ; For all Parochial Purposes, $3,066.84 ; Total Offerings, $3,333.83.

In Sept. the sum of $800 was given by the Rectory Fund Society towards payment of mortgage debt; remainder loaned by Mr. C. F. Brooks, free of interest.

Nov. 16th. The Free Seat System adopted on motion in Vestry meeting, (the proposition having been previously submitted at a meeting of parishioners,) to take effect Easter, 1880.

A. D. 1880. Parochial Report, May 18th, showed Confirmed, 14 ; Communicants, 122 ; For Current Expenses, $1,711.77 ; For all Parochial Purposes, $3,656.19 ; Total Contributions, $3,879.85.

A. D. 1883. The withdrawal of an annual subscription of $500, pledged by Mr. C. F. Brooks upon the adoption of the Free Seat System, led to much financial stringency in this and the following year.

A. D. 1885. May 19th, Parochial Report showed confirmed, 9 ; Communicants, 128 ; For Current Expenses, $1,297.75 ; For all Parochial Purposes, $1,660.79 ; Total of Contributions, $1,855.75.

June 7th and 14th. At meetings of the congregation, held after service, subscriptions were begun by which the floating debt of $611.35 was paid in full, and the $500 mortgage upon the Rectory was also discharged, largely by the liberality of Mr. Edwin Beers, of Brooklyn.

Sept. 17th. The Rev. N. Barrows tendered his resignation, which was accepted with deep regret.

Oct. 22nd. The Rev. Theodore M. Peck, of Piermont, N. Y. was called to the rectorship, with salary of $1,000 per annum, and use of Rectory.

Dec. 11th. The Rev. Theodore M. Peck formally instituted as Rector by the Rev. Dr. Middleton, of Glen Cove, acting for the Bishop of Long Island.

A. D. 1886. May 18th. Parochial Report showed Communicants, 137 ; For Current Expenses, $1,774.81 ; For all Parochial Purposes, $4,214.69 : Total of Contributions, $4,344.23.

This report also makes mention of the great loss of the parish in the departure hence, during the year, of Rufus Prime and Henry J. Scudder, both Vestrymen, and faithful and liberal parishioners. Also, of the starting of a permanent "Endowment Fund" with the offertory ($18.75) on the Sunday of the Rector's Institution.

The church edifice had been repainted and the cross gilded, at a cost of $105, and a building was purchased and refitted for a barn for the Rectory Grounds, at an expense of $225.

On Nov. 1st, All Saints' Day, the first of a line of shade trees, on the lane leading from Main street to the Church, was planted by Miss Nina Prime, in memory of her father; appropriate services being conducted by the Rector, assisted by the Rev. N. Barrows.

On the same day, at Evening Prayer in the Church, "the handsome and Churchly Book-case for the Parish Memorial Library was unveiled, and solemnly set apart for church use with a service of Benediction."

This Library was founded on the Festival of St. Michael and All Angels as a memorial of ISABELLA GIBSON BARROWS, wife of the Rev. N. Barrows, to perpetuate her memory and her influence."

A. D. 1887. The roof of the church building repaired at a cost of $175, and a Fund for the erection of a Sunday School Building or Parish House was begun with an offering of $55.61.

A. D. 1888. No election of Wardens &c., at the usual time, Monday in Easter week, because no electors atttended.

Parochial Report, May 15th, showed Confirmed, 9 ; Communicants, 123 ; For Current Expenses, $1,727.88 ; All Parochial Purposes, $2,032.85 ; Total Contributions, $2,348.42. Trinity Mission, Northport, was reported flourishing, and nearly ready to be set off as a Parish. At Huntington Harbor, Mission Services had been held continuously since St. Andrew's Day, 1887.

At a Vestry Meeting in May, the salary of the Rector was increased to $1,200 per annum, and an appropriation of $500 was made for Organist and Choir. Testimonials of Edgar L. Sanford, Deacon, and Candidate for Priest's Orders, and of Wm. Stanley Barrows, for the Diaconate, were duly signed.

The west end of the Church was this year repaired and replastered. And, largely through the interest and exertions of Mrs. C. P. Holmes, a new carpet was laid within the rail, and a floor of decorated tiles in the Choir.

A. D. 1889. Parochial Report, May 21st, showed Confirmed, 7 : Communicants, 136 : For Current Expenses, $1,451.36 : All Parochial Purposes, $2,669.79 : Total Contributions, $2,889.33. During the year, the improvements already noted had been made, a Building at the Harbor, being a Barn on the Meade property, had been given for a chapel, and adapted to its new use at a cost of $200 ; and $300 had been spent on the Rectory in repairing and painting, and the purchase of a new furnace. A gift is also recorded of a handsome Alms-Bason and Plates " to the Glory of God, and in loving memory of Gertrude B. Hurd, Easter, 1889."

Choir Appropriation this year, or Salary of Organist, $300.

A. D. 1890. Parochial Report, May 20th, showed Confirmed, 12 : Communicants, 151 : For Current Expenses, $1,863.03 : All Parochial Purpose, $2,559.58 : Total Offerings, $2,863.48. The Harbor Chapel had been enlarged, at a cost of $140.

At a Vestry Meeting on June 7th, a resolution was passed abandoning the Free Seat System, and ordering pews offered for rental.

At some time during the Summer the plan of a " Parish Guild " was submitted and accepted, its object being to systematize and bring into organic union the various Societies and

working forces of the Parish.   The first quarterly meeting was
held on St. Luke's Day, Oct. 18th.

A. D. 1891.   Parochial Report, May 19th, showed Confirmed, 9 : Communicants, 149 : For Current Expenses,
$2,183.72 : All Parochial Purposes, $3,046.41 ; Total Contributions, $3,279.04.

Early in October, and at the completion of six years of energetic and successful labor, the Rev. Theo. M. Peck resigned
the rectorship, his resignation to take effect Nov. 1st.

On the latter date, his successor, the Rev. Chas. W. Tur\
ner, formerly of St. Matthew's Church, Brooklyn, and for the
last two years Dean of St. Matthew's Cathedral, Dallas, Texas,
took charge of the parish.

A. D. 1892.   Report, May 17th, showed Communicants,
146 ; Current Expenses, $1,700.00 ; Total Parochial Purposes,
$2,362.54 ; Total of Contributions, $2,445.17.

A. D. 1893.   Report, May 16th, showed Confirmations,
16 : Communicants, 151 : Current Expenses, $1,965.11 ; Total
for Parochial Purposes, $2,828.87 ; Total Contributions,
$3,093.02.

A D 1894.   Report to May 16th, showed Confirmations,
16 : Communicants, 144 : Current Expenses, $1,824.57 : Total
for Parochial Purposes, $2,483.84 : Total Contributions,
$2,673.44.

Soon afterwards, a Water Motor was purchased and attached to the Organ at a total expense of $250.

Rectors of this Parish

And others who have had definite official relation
as Missionaries, &c.

1745 to 1764.	Rev. Samuel Seabury, Rector of St. George's, Hempstead, Missionary and Founder.
1748 to 1752.	Mr. Samuel Seabury, afterwards Rt. Rev. Bishop Seabury, Catechist or Lay-Reader.
1764 to 1765.	Mr. Ebenezer Kneeland, (subsequently ordained) Reader.
1769 to 1773.	Rev. James Greaton, Rector.
1789.	Rev. Andrew Fowler, Missionary.
1805.	Rev. John C. Rudd, Missionary.
1814 to 1823.	Rev. Chas. Seabury, of Caroline Church, Setauket, in charge.
1823 to 1826.	Rev. Edward K. Fowler, Deacon and Missionary.
1826 to 1827.	Rev. Samuel Seabury, Deacon and Missionary.
1834 to 1838.	Rev. Isaac Sherwood, of St. John's Cold Spring
1838 to 1843.	Harbor. In first period, Missionary, subsequently Rector.
1843 to 1844.	Rev. Moses Marcus, Rector.
1845 to 1847.	Rev. Chas. H. Hall, Rector.

1847 to 1848.	Rev. C. Donald MacLeod, Rector.
1848 to 1850.	Rev. Fred W. Shelton, Rector.
1852 to 1856.	Rev. W. A. W. Maybin, Rector.
1856 to 1858.	Rev. Wm. G. Farrington, Rector.
1858 to 1859.	Rev. J. H. Williams, Rector.
1859 to 1860.	Rev. Wm. J. Lynd, Rector.
1860 to 1870.	Rev. Caleb B. Ellsworth, Rector.
1871 to 1877.	Rev. A. J. Barrow, Rector.
1877 to 1878.	Rev. Thaddeus H. Snively, Rector.
1878 to 1885.	Rev. N. Barrows, Rector.
1885 to 1891.	Rev. Theo. M. Peck Rector.
1891.	Rev. Chas. W. Turner, Rector.

The fact that the REV. SAMUEL SEABURY, of Hempstead, was the Founder of this parish, and that successive sons in one line of his distinguished descendants to the fourth generation have all officiated here, three of them having been also, at some time in their ministry, in direct official relation with the parish, renders it fitting that some detailed notice should here be given of his life and missionary labors; as also, afterwards, of those of his venerated son, the first Bishop of the American Church.

REV. SAMUEL SEABURY, the elder, was born in Groton, —now Ledyard,—Conn., in 1706. His ancestors were of Portlake, Devonshire, Eng. It has been affirmed that the ancient form of the name was Sedborough or Seaberry. He was a grandson of Samuel Seabury, a noted physician and surgeon of

Duxbury, Mass., and the son of a man of prominence among the Congregationalists of New London.

In Mr. Seabury's early manhood he officiated as a licensed preacher to the Congregationalists, but says Sprague, (in Epis. Pulpit p. 149) was never Congregationally ordained. He had been a student at Yale College at that memorable period when the Congregational "standing order" were astonished and angered by the announcement of Dr. Cutler, the President of the College, that he had become an Episcopalian. In the strife and confusion which arose in consequence of this avowal, Mr. Seabury found his studies interrupted, and therefore transferred himself to Harvard University, where he graduated in 1724.

He married Abigail Mumford, a relative of his Episcopal neighbor, the Rev. Dr. McSparran, Rector of the Episcopal Church at Narragansett, R. I. This lady was the mother of Bishop Seabury. She died in 1731, and in 1733 Mr. Seabury took as his second wife Elizabeth, daughter of Adam Powell, a merchant of Newport, R. I. She survived her husband many years and attained a venerable age, dying at Hempstead in 1799. Mr. Seabury's grandmother was Elizabeth Alden, a descendant of John Alden, said to have been the first man that landed on Plymouth Rock.

In the spring of 1730, Mr. Seabury, leaving his family at home, took passage for England for the purpose of seeking Episcopal ordination. He carried with him letters of commendation from the Rev. Dr. Timothy Cutler, of Christ Church, Boston, and from the Rev. Dr. McSparran, of Narragansett.

The application for Orders was successful: Mr. Seabury was ordained Deacon, and shortly afterwards, Priest, probably by the Bishop of London. And on the 21st of August, 1730, he appeared before the Venerable Society, and after due examination and enquiry, was appointed. Missionary to New London, Conn. Soon afterwards he preached in St. Michael's Church, Cornhill, from the 1st Ep. to the Thess., v. xvii, "Pray without ceasing." This sermon, still in the possession of his descendants, shows Mr. S. to have been a preacher of great earnestness, directness of address, a devout spirit, and an excellent logician. These traits are manifested perhaps still more forcibly in another sermon preached by him at this period, in which he maintains, with great lucidity in the arrangement and statement of his argument, that the use of a Liturgy and prescribed forms of prayer are both Scriptural and best adapted to the spiritual needs of men in public worship.

Returning to this country in 1732, Mr. Seabury commenced his labors in New London, as the first minister of St. James' Church where, for the succeeding ten years, he prosecuted the duties of his calling with assiduity and with an encouraging degree of success. Before leaving New London for St. George's, Hempstead, he preached a sermon which was "published at the desire of some who heard it."

The few productions of Mr. Seabury's pen which have been preserved make us regret that he did not publish more. They show that he was a man of no ordinary mental capacity. He took hold of subjects with a firm grasp, and treated them with vigorous common sense, and was able to convey the impression that he was himself thoroughly convinced of those things of which he sought to convince others.

Of Mr. Seabury's personal appearance an aged parishioner of St. George's Church gave to his rector (Dr. Moore) the following representation : " My father described him to me as, " seated upon a strong sorrel horse he made his way to Oyster " Bay and Huntington, with his saddle bags strapped to his " saddle. He was strongly built, but not tall, and he had " a countenance which was intelligent and kindly, and showed " decision and firmness. He wore a three-cornered hat, and " small clothes and top-boots. He rode well, but sometimes " could not make the journey in time to have service and re- " turn the same day."

At the time Mr. Seabury became the minister of Hemp- stead, the labors and influence of his predecessors, Thomas and Jenney, had begun to bring forth increasing good fruits, a re- compense to their devoted efforts. Prejudices and enmities has nearly expended themselves. Most of the inveterate opposers had died. A more tolerant and intelligent generation occupied their places ; and the services of the Church were not only ac- cepted but even sought after in all directions.

Mr. Seabury, who evidently possessed a most vigorous constitution, endeavored to improve every opening : and the church records show that his ministrations were extended not only to all parts of Queen's County east of Jamaica and to Hunt- ington township in Suffolk, but also to many places in West- chester and even in Dutchess county. Having visited the lat- ter, in response to an appeal from residents there, and finding the people very eager for the services of the Church, he repeated his visits, and after a time, by the direction of the Venerable Society, formally took them under his pastoral care, although one might think he was already well burdened. Among the places in which official acts are recorded as having been done by him in that county mention is made of Poughkeepsie, Fishkill, Phillipsborough, Nine-Partners, Rumbout, Bateman's Precinct and Crom-Elbow.

Mr. Seabury, like every minister of the Church in North America, became increasingly sensible of the evil and anomaly of the Church not being provided with a Bishop ; he felt constrained to address a letter to the Bishop of London in 1753, urging that a Bishop be consecrated for the American Colonies. But the Church was hindered by politicians, and these cared not if three out of every ten candidates for ordination who sailed for England died either of small-pox or by shipwreck.

Faithful and unremitting in his labors as Mr. Seabury was, the people did not very generously support him, and therefore, in addition to his "care of all the churches," he was compelled to resort to teaching. He built a school house in the rear of the Parsonage, and boarded some of his pupils in his own house "at £30 per year, schooling, washing, and wood for school fire included." The school obtained much repute, and was attended by the children of many prominent families whose names have become historic.

Mr. Seabury had marked success in bringing persons to baptism. He reported on March 26th 1762, the baptism of eleven adults, who all appeared properly affected on the occasion. "One of them, particularly, Joseph Cheeseman, de-"clared publicly, that it was after considering most other pro-"fessions, and upon mature deliberation, he had determined to "make the solemn confession of his faith" in the Church of "England; and accordingly, himself, his wife, and eight "children were baptized."

During the twenty-two years of Mr. Seabury's ministry in Hempstead, he baptized 1,071 persons. A number of

these are recorded to have been baptized "by immersion."
He was, indeed, in the proper sense of the term "a Bap-
tist." The parish records show that he remitted none of
his labors to the very end of his life. He was constantly
passing from point to point in his extended field of labor,
seeking to win souls to Christ : and his utter forgetfulness
of self cannot but have mitigated towards him the opposi-
tion of which he had so often to make mention.

In the midst of his faithful endeavors his career was
brought to a close. Having taken a voyage to England in
June, 1763, probably to seek surgical aid, he returned in
1764, in the language of his wife "a sick—a dying man."
In a newspaper of that day appeared the following notice of
his death :—"Rev. Mr. Seabury died of a nervous disorder
"and an imposthume in his side, June 15, 1764, aged 58 ; a gen-
"tleman of amiable, exemplary character, greatly and generally
"beloved and lamented."

His remains lie interred in St. George's churchyard, and
the stone at the head of his grave has this inscription :—

> Here lyeth interred the body of the
> Rev. Sam'l. Seabury, A. M.
> Rector of the parish of Hempstead,
> Who with the greatest diligence
> And most indefatigable labour,
> For 13 years at New-London,
> And 21 years in this parish,
> Having discharged every duty
> Of his sacred functions ;
> Died the 15th of June A. D. 1764, Aet. 58.
> In gratitude to the memory of the best of husbands
> His disconsolate widow, Elizabeth Seabury,
> Hath placed this stone.

The foregoing account of the life and labors of the Rev. Samuel Seabury, the elder, is largely worded as given in the late Dr. Moore's History of St. George's Hempstead; but is abridged and re-arranged, as events special to that parish stated there in order of their occurrence could here be omitted.

In order, however, that a fair impression may be given of the mingled steadfastness and gentleness of Mr. Seabury's character, as also of the circumstances attending the beginning of his labors here, one additional fact must be stated, or rather alluded to, which is given more particularly in Dr. Moore's work, but which the present writer would willingly have passed over in entire silence if such silence had been consistent with justice.

Though prejudices against this Church still linger in many of our rural communities, and though misapprehensions as to her origin, her mind and ways are not uncommon, yet in our day her representatives receive as a rule nothing but kindness, and are accorded everywhere not only a free field but a welcome. In Seabury's day it was different. To religious toleration, as people understand it now, Dissenters or Non-conformists, as they were then called, (and as they are still called, and call themselves, in England,) were no more inclined in reality than were Churchmen of the days of the Tudors and the Stuarts. The former conscientiously believed that they had the more scriptural system; and they wanted "freedom to worship God" in that way. But they thought that others also should worship God in *that same way*; and they had no notion of willingly allowing them to do anything else. The design of the Puritans and others was the settlement and maintenance here of a new and, as they thought, a better, ecclesiastical rule and system, purged of the taint of the old church; and therefore it is not perhaps surprising that anything that threatened to interfere with that design was as far as possible resisted. Apparently Mr. Seabury was able even then to make this charitable allowance for the bitter words which were spoken, and even for the personal denunciations with which he was assailed. He rendered not "evil for evil or railing for railing," nor would he be drawn into acrimonious controversy. In calm and gentle terms he declared his purpose simply "to prosecute the commission and command" which he had received "to preach repentance and remission of sins in the Master's Name."

We do not know anything as to the immediate effect of this answer, but its worthiness, so far at least as regards tone and temper, will cheerfully be acknowledged, doubtless, by all. And it is a fairly representative statement of the position throughout of the ministry to which Seabury belonged ; which regards itself, not as free to please itself or to conform itself to the demands of local public opinion as shaped by the influences and information of any particular time, but as being " under authority," with definite obligations and definite responsibilities. Its main and proper concern is simply to do the work of the Church to which it is responsible in her own quiet way.

SAMUEL SEABURY, son of the Missionary at Hempstead, was fourteen years of age at the time of his father's removal to Long Island—having been born in Groton, Conn., Nov. 30th, 1729. He was distinguished from his youth for soundness of mind and solidity of judgment, and gave early promise of future usefulness. When the elder Seabury extended his labors from Hempstead to Huntington, he requested the Missionary Society in England to appoint his son as Catechist and Reader. Such

was the modest commencement of a long series of services to
the Church by the future Bishop of Connecticut. He had graduated at Yale College in 1748, was appointed to Huntington the
same year, and, after serving for about three years under his
father's direction, went to Edinburgh in 1751 to study medicine.

Yet, although the Episcopal Church in Scotland was in
very "low estate," caution having to be used even in attending her services, which appear to have been held in upper
rooms of obscure houses, Mr. Seabury was soon moved to de-
vote himself to the ministry, entered upon his preparatory
studies with all vigor, and was ordained by Dr. Sherlock,
Bishop of London, in 1753.

On his return to America, Mr. Seabury was appointed by
the Society for the Propagation of the Gospel as Missionary at
New Brunswick, N. J., where he began his labors on May 25th,
1754. The young clergyman was received with a hearty welcome by the people, and the stone church, which he found
nearly finished, was soon filled. Here he remained until Easter,
1757, when he received an appointment from the Governer of the
Province of New York as minister of Grace church, Jamaica, in
Queen's County, a pastorate which then included Newtown
and Flushing. Here he was rector from 1757 to 1766. He
had married on Oct. 12th, 1756, Mary, daughter of Edward
Hicks. He had "the more readily removed to Jamaica as it
"brought him nearer to a most excellent father whom he
"dearly loved, and whose conversation he highly valued."*

The elder Seabury died on the 15th of June, 1764, while
his son was rector at Jamaica. Shortly before, Mr. Ebenezer

*From History of the Church in Jamaica, by the late H. Onder-
donk, Jr.

Kneeland, Catechist, had been transferred from Flushing to Huntington, but after about a year's service went to England for Orders, and on his return settled at Stratford, Conn., where he died in 1777. So that Huntington as well as Hempstead was vacant, and it is not unlikely that Mr. Seabury, who writes in 1765 that he has supplied the vacant church at Hempstead as often as he could, may also have re-visited Huntington.

On Dec. 3rd, 1766, Mr. Seabury, with consent of the Venerable Society to his removal from Jamaica, was instituted rector of St. Peter's church, Westchester. In the following decade, the revolutionary troubles began, and Mr. Seabury, with conscientious firmness, held fast to his allegiance to the mother country. He had to endure, therefore, with some others of the clergy, much odium and suffering for a course of conduct which, whatever may be thought of it by others, they themselves believed to be right. In 1776, he was seized and carried to New Haven, Conn., where he was cast into prison. But the suspicion under which he rested could not be satisfactorily established and he was finally dismissed, and returned to his parish. Subsequently, however, his church was converted into a hospital by the American soldiers, and he with difficulty made his escape to Long Island, supporting himself and his family, during the remainder of the war, by the practice of medicine in New York.

When the final issue declared America triumphant, the Church which had been bound to that of the old country by so many tender ties was left impoverished and almost desolate. But her clergy and laity who in the face of popular odium remained faithful, and who esteemed their heritage in her as too precious to be lost, soon girded themselves to meet the new needs, and before the British troops, with reluctant steps, had left New York, the Episcopal clergy of Connecticut held a private meeting in the city, and elected the Rev. Jeremiah Leaming, D. D., as their choice to be Bishop of Connecticut. When he declined, on account of advancing years, the Rev. Samuel Seabury, D. D. was, on the 21st of April, 1783, unanimously chosen.

The story of the fruitless negotiations with the authorities of the Church of England, who were hampered by the delicate political situation, as also of the appeal, finally successful, to the Scottish Bishops, of Seabury's memorable consecration and his fruitful Episcopate, are matters of general church history. All that can here be stated is that he was consecrated on Nov. 14th, 1784, by Bishops Kilgour, Petrie, and Skinner; and that, returning to America in 1785, he settled at New London, Connecticut, where he soon after entered upon the double duty of the Rectorship of St. James' Church in that place, and of the Episcopate of Connecticut.

The most active and useful life must have an end, and the summons to cease from earthly labors sometimes comes suddenly. It was so with Bishop Seabury. He had entered upon his sixty-sixth year, but continued to discharge the duties of his parish and diocese with all the devotion and zeal of earlier days. On the 25th of February, 1796, however, after an evening spent at the house of a friend, on returning to the parsonage, he was suddenly seized with apoplexy and expired. The first resting place of his body was in the churchyard of St. James', New London, but upon the completion of the beautiful church there, his remains were removed and buried beneath the chancel. The inscription on the tomb is as follows :

The
Rt. Rev. Father in God,
SAMUEL SEABURY, D. D.
First Bishop of Connecticut
And of the Prot. Episc. Church in the U. S.
Consecrated Aberdeen, Scotland, Nov. 1784
Died February 25th, 1796, aged 67.
The Diocese of Connecticut recorded here
its grateful memory of his virtues and services.

A. D. 1849.

The following is a part of the inscription upon the old monument, which yet remains in the graveyard of St. James' Church :—

" Ingenuous without pride, learned without pedantry,
" good without severity ; he was duly qualified to discharge
" the duties of the Christian and the Bishop.   In the pulpit he
" enforced religion, in his conduct he exemplified it.   The poor
" he assisted with his charity, the ignorant he blessed with his
" instruction.   The friend of men, he ever devised their good ;
" the enemy of vice, he ever opposed it.   Christian, dost thou
" aspire to happiness?   Seabury has shown the way that leads
" to it."—(*Chiefly from the "Life of Bishop Seabury" by the
Rev. John N. Norton.*)

REV. JAMES GREATON, 1769 to 1773.   Specially notable because he was the first rector or resident pastor ; because the parish when bereaved of him encountered trying times which deprived it of settled priestly functions for a period of fifty years ; and because his rectorship though brief, covering apparently, less than four years, was evidently happy and fruitful, his work receiving the commendation of the Venerable Society, from which he held appointment as Missionary.   Allusion to his earlier life and ministry will be found in the Historical Note by the Rev. C. B. Ellsworth, page 72.

To those who at intervals ministered here as Missionaries during the fifty years following Mr. Greaton's rectorship, as also to the REV. EDWARD K. FOWLER, and the REV. SAMUEL SEABURY, serving in succession as Missionaries from 1823 to 1827, reference is made in the " Annals."

REV. ISAAC SHERWOOD was rector at the time of the Incorporation of the parish in 1838, resigned in 1843, when the parish voted to dispense with missionary aid. Continued in charge of the Church at Cold Spring Harbor until his death. " In the " church at that place is a neat mural tablet erected to his mem- " ory, a recognition of virtues and labors which deserve the " grateful remembrance of a Christian people."—(Rev. C. B. Ellsworth.)

REV. MOSES MARCUS. Resigned 1844. Became rector of St. George the Martyr, in New York. Died in England.

REV. CHAS. H. HALL, D. D. Made Deacon on the 12th Sunday after Trinity, 1844, at Tivoli on the Hudson. Took charge here April 13th, 1845. Ordained to the Priesthood the same year. Left Huntington at Easter, 1847, for the Church of the Holy Innocents at Highland Falls, near West Point. Took charge of St. John's Church, John's Island, S. C., Nov. 27th, 1848. Rector of Church of the Epiphany, Washington, D. C., from 1857 to 1869. Has been Rector of the church of the Holy Trinity, Brooklyn, N. Y., since March 1st, 1869.

REV. C. DONALD MACLEOD. Resigned in 1848. Afterwards became a Romanist. Date of death not known.

REV. FREDERICK WILLIAM SHELTON, L.L. D., was a native of Jamaica, L. I., his father being a Presbyterian Elder. Graduated at the College of New Jersey, and spent a year as teacher in the Episcopal school at Raleigh, N. C. Entered the Gen. Theological Seminary, where he graduated in 1847. Was admitted to Deacon's Orders the same year. Became rector of this parish, resigning probably in 1850. Was subsequently rector of Trinity Church, Fishkill, N. Y., and of Christ Church, Montpelier, Vermont. Honorary degree of L.L. D. conferred by Middlebury College, Vt.

The following works from his pen were published : The Trollopiad, a Satirical Poem, in 1837 ; The Gold Mania, and The Use and Abuse of Reason, Lectures, in 1850 ; Salander and the Dragon, a Romance, in 1851 ; The Rector of St. Bardolph's, a well known work, 1852, republished 1856 ; Up the River, 1853 ; Chrystalline, a Romance, 1854 ; Peeps from a Belfry, 1855. He was also a frequent contributor to the Knickerbocker and other Magazines.

Dr. Shelton was an amiable, genial, lovable man ; a fine scholar ; his style was distinguished for its classic purity ; he delighted in the beauties of nature and of art, and was capable of appreciating them. He hated shams, and his satires were full of quiet scathing rebukes of mere pretension. As a pastor, he always won the love and respect of his people. He died at Carthage Landing, N. Y., June 20th, (year not named.)—(Extracts from an Obituary Notice.)

REV. W. A. W. MAYBIN. Resigned in 1856. Became Rector of St. Paul's Church, Brooklyn, E. D. Died at Wilmington, Del., July 18th, 1887, aged 62.

REV. WM. G. FARRINGTON, D. D.   Ordered deacon in Trinity church, New York, on St. Peter's Day 1856, by Bishop Horatio Potter; assisted in Church of the Transfiguration, New York; became rector of St. John's Church, Huntington, Nov. 2nd, 1856; advanced to the priesthood by Bishop Potter on St. Thomas' Day the same year; resigned rectorship of this parish, July 4th, 1858; by appointment of the rector of Trinity Church, New York, assisted in that parish from Dec. 15th, 1858 to Easter, 1862; organized Christ Church, Hackensack, N. J., April 12th, 1863, and became rector of the same Oct. 15th, the same year; was married Jan. 14th, 1865, to Anna Wilson Kip, daughter of Leonard W. Kip, Esq., of New York; resigned rectorship of Christ Church, Hackensack, April 30th, 1870, and on Whitsunday, the same year, entered upon the rectorship of St. Barnabas' Church, Newark, N. J., which he held until Easter, 1872; was in charge of the Church of the Holy Innocents, St. Cloud, West Orange, N. J., from May 1st, 1872 to April 1st, 1877; in 1872 received the honorary degree of Doctor of Divinity from the College of William and Mary; was rector of Christ Church, Bloomfield, N. J., from April 1st, 1877 to Sept. 30th, 1889; Sept. 1st, 1889, became a member of the Editorial Staff of *The Churchman* of New York, which position he still holds

REV. JAMES H. WILLIAMS.   Resigned in 1859. Afterwards rector of Zion Church, Greenburgh, N. Y.   His last residence was in the City of New York, with a Summer home near Lynchburg, Va., where he died, in or near the year 1889.

REV. WM. J. LYND.   Mr. Lynd became interested in the early history of the parish, wrote a paper concerning it, and went to Albany to enquire about the lost glebe. Was informed that the land could not be recovered. Resigned in 1860. Became rector of St. Barnabas' Church, Newark, N. J. In 1867 entered upon Missionary work in Colorado, Wyoming and New Mexico. In 1883 engaged in Missionary work in Northern California. Owing to defective eyesight, has not been in active service in late years. Resides in Oakland, Cal.

REV. CALEB B. ELLSWORTH, was a valued member of the Missionary Committee of the diocese. After an active rectorship of ten years, resigned in 1870. Became rector of St. Saviour's, Maspeth, L. I. Died in 1891.

REV. ALFRED J. BARROW, entered upon the work of the ministry at Harrisburg, Pa., in 1864; subsequently laid the foundations of St. James' Parish, Bedford Springs; became rector of this parish, May 1st, 1871; resigned June 1st, 1877, to accept the rectorship of the Church of the Atonement, Brooklyn, N. Y., serving there until Dec. 1st, 1879, when he undertook some special missionary work in Central Pennsylvania; on Feb. 1st, 1881, accepted a call to St. John's, Baltimore and Harford Counties, Md.; in December 1883, was called to St. Peter's, Bennington, Vermont, where he remained until July, 1887. After a visit to Europe and a year spent in Missouri was laid aside for a considerable time with cataract and had an operation performed. On May 1st, 1890, took charge of St. James' Parish, Lower Providence, Pa., thirty miles from Philadelphia, and of a Mission at Royersford.

REV. THADDEUS A. SNIVELY, resigned in 1878. Became rector of St. John's Church, Troy, N. Y. Now rector of St. Chrysostom's, Chicago, Ill.

REV. N. BARROWS, was for several years a member of the Standing Committee of the diocese. Resigned in 1885. Became rector of Christ Church, Short Hills, N. J. where he now is.

REV. THEO. M. PECK, resigned in 1891. Became Missionary in charge of the N. E. Convocation district, Diocese of Connecticut, with headquarters at Putnam, Ct. where he now is.

REV. CHAS. WM. TURNER. Graduated at St. Marks' College, Chelsea, London, England, July, 1864. Master at the Normal school there until Nov. 1866. Admitted to Deacon's Orders early in 1867. Master of St. Alban's School, Honolulu, Hawaii, until Sept. 1869. Assistant at Trinity Church, San Francisco, Cal. Nov. 1869, and in charge of that parish the greater part of the year following. Ordained Priest Nov. 1870. In May 1878, became rector of St. Paul's, Oakland, Cal. Came East Sept. 1874, and in Nov. of the same year, rector of St. John's church, Long Island City. Rector of St. Matthew's, Brooklyn, from Nov. 1876 to Oct. 1889. For two years rector of St. Matthew's Parish, Dallas, Texas, and Dean of the Cathedral. Became rector of St. John's, Huntington, Nov. 1st, 1891.

Church Wardens of this Parish,

With their Terms of Service.

ADAMS, ISAAC, 1886.

BARR, GEORGE F., 1890.

CAMBRELING, CHURCHILL C., 1843, 1844, 1856.

CROSSMAN, FRANK M., 1875 to 1878.

DOVING, IRA E., 1879 to 1884.

DUSENBERRY, EDWIN B., 1891 to present time.

HAWTHORN, WILLIAM M., 1853, 1854.

HURD, ARTHUR T., 1875 to 1889.

HOLDEN, HENRY W., 1885, 1886.

JONES, JOHN, 1788 to 1790.

JOHNSON, JOHN, 1791 to 1800.

*KISSAM DANIEL W., 1800 to 1805, 1838.

KISSAM, EDWARD, 1868 to 1870.

LEFFORD, ADAM, 1788 to 1790.

NICOLL, WM., 1864 to 1867.

POST, RICHARD B., 1855, 1862, 1863.

PAULDING, HIRAM, JR., 1871 to 1874, 1885, 1886.

RHINELANDER, DR. JOHN R., 1838 to 1853.

RAY, DR. JOSEPH, 1845 to 1853, 1856 to 1865.

SMITH, SHUBAEL, 1793 to 1805.

STOUT, WILLIAM C., 1840 to 1843, 1856 to 1861.

SCHMIDT, OSCAR EGERTON, 1887 to present time.

WILLIAMS, GILBERT, 1866 to 1871.

YOUNGS, DANIEL K., 1872 to 1874.

*Doct. Daniel Whitehead Kissam, son of Joseph and Mary (Hewlett) Kissam, was born at Great Neck, L. I., March 23rd, 1763. He received his medical education under the tuition of Dr. Bayley of New York, and was a fellow student with the late Drs. Mitchell and Post, of that city. He commenced the practice of medicine at Glen Cove, and after the death of Dr. Sanford removed to this village, where he continued his practice nearly forty years. As a physician, he was skilful, attentive, and faithful. As a citizen, he was distinguished for his integrity, punctuality and independence. He was ardently attached to the Episcopal Church of this village, and was its main supporter for many years in its languishing condition. Dr. Kissam was attacked by disease in 1830 with which he lingered until 1839, when he died, aged 76 years.

Vestrymen of this Parish,

With their terms of Service.

ADAMS, ISAAC, 1853, 1856 to 1869.
ATWATER, ELISHA M., 1858 to 1862.
ALSOP, JOHN, 1863.
ACKERMAN, GEORGE B., 1865 to 1868.
BLOODGOOD, NATHANIEL, 1838.
BRYAR, EDWARD K., 1856.
BARR GEORGE F., 1879 to 1881, 1883 to present time.
BRONSON, WILLETT, 1880 to 1887.
BERRIAN, CHAS. A., 1882, 1883.
CONKLIN, ELKANAH, 1804, 1805.
CONKLIN, JOSEPH O., 1843.
CAMBRELING, CHURCHILL C., 1842 to 1848, 1855 to 1858
CROSSMAN, FRANK M., 1868 to 1874.
CAIRE, JOHN S., 1877 to 1880.
DOUGLAS, LEMUEL, 1795 to 1797.
DOYING, IRA E., 1872 to 1878.
DERBY, DR. RICHARD H., 1883, 1884, 1887 to present time
DUSENBERRY, EDWIN B., 1889, 1890.
ECKERSON, M. B., 1872.
FORDHAM, AUSTIN S., 1845, 1846.
FLEET, CHAS. H., 1848 to 1873.
HEWLETT, WM., 1838.
HAWTHORN, WM. M., 1838 to 1848, 1855, 1856.
HURD, ARTHUR T., 1872 to 1874.
HOLDEN, HENRY W., 1875 to 1884, 1887, 1888.
HURD, RUSSELL, 1885.
HOLMES, CHAS. P., 1889 to 1891.
IRWIN, JAMES D., 1871.
IRWIN, JOSEPH, 1877 to present time
JOHNSON, JOHN, 1758 to 1790.
JOHNSON, WM., 1789, 1795, 1796.
JOHNSON, JOHN, JR., 1797 to 1803.
JOHNSON, JACOB, 1804, 1805.
JONES, SAMUEL W., 1872 to 1877.

JOHNSON, CHAS. S., 1890,

KISSAM, EDWARD, 1864 to 1867.

KISSAM, AUGUSTUS, 1882,

LEFFORD, ADAM, 1800 to 1805.

LONG, HEWLETT J., 1861, 1862, 1866 to 1871, 1887 to present time.

LORD, THOMAS, JR., 1875, 1876.

MEADE, RICHARD W., 1878.

MASON, THOMAS, 1892 to present time.

NICOLL, WM., 1860 to 1863.

PLATT, JOEL, 1835.

PAULDING, HIRAM, 1838.

POST, RICHARD B., 1839 to 1848, 1853, 1857, 1858.

PIERSON, ——— 1840.

*PRIME, RUFUS, 1863 to 1866, 1870 to 1882.

PAULDING, HIRAM, JR., 1867, to 1869, 1881, 1884.

PLATT, HENRY C., 1881 to 1884, 1890 to present time.

RAY, DR. JOSEPH, 1839 to 1845.

ROWLAND, JONATHAN, 1842.

ROWELL, WM. L., 1844.

ROGERS, STEPHEN C., 1862 to 1880.

STEWART, CHAS. T., 1838.

STOUT WM. C., 1838, 1839, 1845, 1846, 1855.

SCUDDER, HENRY, 1840 to 1842.

SCUDDER, HENRY T., 1846, 1855 to 1860.

SMALLWOOD, DR. SAM'L B., 1869 to 1871.

SCHMIDT, OSCAR E., 1884 to 1886.

SCUDDER, EDWARD M., 1884 to 1889.

SIMPSON, WM., 1885, 1886.

THURSTON, LEWIS M., 1840 to 1846, 1855, 1856, 1863, 1867 to 1870.

THURSTON, WM., 1874, 1875.

THURSTON, CHAS. S., 1876.

VAN WYCK, ABRAHAM, 1835 to 1844.

VAN WYCK, SAMUEL, 1842 to 1846.

VAN WYCK, SAMUEL A., 1870.

VAN SCHAICK, EDWIN, 1891 to present time.

WIGGINS, DANIEL, 1790.

WOOD, STEPHEN, 1839, to 1842.

*Mr. Rufus Prime was elected Warden in 1875, but declined the honor, accepting however, the office of Vestryman, in which he had served before, and to which he was re-elected.

WILLIAMS. GILBERT. 1844 to 1848, 1855 to 1865.
WEST, WILLIAM, 1855 to 1865, 1871 to 1874, 1884, 1885.
WELLS, JOHN J., 1863, 1864.
WOOD, WILTON W., 1885 to present time.
YOUNGS, ISAAC. 1758,
YOUNGS, DANIEL K., 1866 to 1869.
YOUNG. THOMAS. 1875 to 1883.

Mame of the Church.

The following brief extract from a letter of H. Lloyd, (2nd,) dated Boston, Nov. 20th, 1764, addressed to his brother Joseph Lloyd, at Queen's Village, seems to show that up to that date, nearly twenty years after the starting of the work, no name had been given to the Church or Parish. The latter had probably been spoken of simply as the Church of England congregation at Huntington.

The extract appears as a postscript to a letter concerning a deed (No. 2) to the Glebe, and is as follows :—

" You'll find blanks left in the deed for the name of the "church. If not already named, it may be as proper, and more "so, to have it called Christ Church, than by any other name."

On this, the late Mr. H. Lloyd (4th) remarks: " The suggestion, it seems, was never acted upon." In fact, there does not seem to have been any definite decision as to the name, for in the deed itself, dated Nov. 21st, one blank is filled by the word " Trinity " but the other blank is left vacant.

Extracts from Notes

Unsigned, but apparently written at the time of the laying of the Corner-Stone of the new church, and probably by Rev. C. B. Ellsworth.

" The materials for a history of this venerable parish are, " so far as known, extremely limited.

" There is a tradition, which I think is entitled to credit, " that at the breaking out of the War of the Revolution, the " early records of this parish were taken by a Mr. Johnson, a " prominent member at that time, to Norwalk, in Connecticut, " along with his own papers for safe keeping during those trou- " blesome times. Having deposited them with a family by the " name of Mott, he departed for a visit to England, but never " returned, having been lost at sea. It is said that his papers " were afterwards destroyed by fire, and probably the Church " papers with them.

" There are therefore no sources of information known at " present, except the records of the Society for the Propagation " of the Gospel in London, Eng., and those of the neighboring " parish at Hempstead, L. I., and oral tradition."

.   .   .   .

Here follows a summary of the successive events, so far as known to the writer, which have been already set forth chrono- logically in this work. Some few matters of interest not mentioned therein are given in the following extracts : —

" Benjamin Treadwell of Hempstead and Phœbe Platt, of " Huntington, united in marriage by the Rev. Mr. Jenney, of

" the former place, in 1727, became the Great-Grand-parents of
" the late Bishops of Pennsylvania and New York."—(Onderdonk.)

" The first settled minister " was " the Rev. James Grea-
" ton, a gentleman from Boston, New England, of good abili-
" ties, prominent family, and ample fortune. He had been
" educated at Yale College, ordained in England, and settled at
" Boston, as the assistant of Rev. Dr. Cutler, the first Rector of
" Christ Church, Boston ; to the rectorship of which he suc-
" ceeded, after the death of Dr. C. He remained in Boston till
" 1767," (should be "1769."—Ed.) when he removed to this
" place and remained till his death in 1773. His remains were
" deposited beneath the chancel of the church in which he min-
" istered."

" In 1801 a charge was made against the parish by the
" Treasurer, John Johnson, for cash paid to Judge Thompson
" to give an account of the annual income."

" In 1806 the church edifice was new roofed by subscrip-
" tion. Prominent among the subscribers were Timothy Wil
" liams, Abial Gould, Richard Budwell, Moses Ralph, Stephen
" Fleet, David Rogers and Jonathan Smith."

" In 1838, the church edifice was partially repaired, and
duly " consecrated to the worship of God by Bishop B. T.
" Onderdonk in 1839."

" In 1843, the Rev. Moses Marcus was elected to the rec-
" torship at a salary of $250 per annum.

" In 1844 the Ladies of the Parish realized from a Fair
" $225, which they devoted towards the purchase of a parson-
" age, and a Committee of three,—Doctors' Ray and Rhinelan-

"der and Gilbert P. Williams, was appointed to purchase a
" parsonage.

" After one year Mr. Marcus resigned the rectorship in
" consequence of the inadequacy of the support. He after-
" wards became the Rector of the Church of St. George the
" Martyr, in N. Y. While on a visit to England, his native
" country, he died. As a scholar, he was thoroughly educated,
" and he was energetic and faithful as a clergyman.

" In 1845 the Rev. Chas. H. Hall entered upon the rec-
" torship. During the first year of his incumbency the church
edifice was thoroughly overhauled and repaired." * * *

" In 1846, the parsonage fund was devoted to the purchase
" of a second-hand organ." (Probably the instrument which,
after 25 years of service here, was given to Grace Church,
Riverhead, and has been in use there for 21 years.—Editor.)

" At Easter 1848 the congregation refused to proceed to
" the election required by statute, but passed a resolution to
" send a petition to the State Legislature praying them to dis-
" solve the corporation of this church."

A very strange resolution, for which no reason is given in
the minutes, and on which, apparently, no action was taken.
—(Editor.)

" The old church was vacated the last Sunday in July,
" 1861, with appropriate services, and the next day the work of
" removing it commenced preparatory to the new.

" In excavating for the basement, the remains of three
" bodies were found beneath the chancel of the old church.
" One was known to be that of the first Rector, Jas. Greaton.
" Of the names of the others, or any circumstances concerning
" them, nothing is known, except the well-defined tradition

" that they were clergymen. Their remains will be decently
" re-interred to-day, under the chancel of the new church at the
" laying of the corner-stone."

The tradition as to the two additional bodies being those
of clergymen is somewhat doubtful. Mr. John W. Greaton,
(grandson of the Rev. James Greaton,) who himself handled
pick and shovel at the excavation, says that there was nothing
in the placing of the bodies to suggest such a conclusion, and
that one of the men having a bullet hole in the skull, had evidently been shot and probably buried where he fell.

The editor has found that the evidence for the various parish traditions that have come to his knowledge is very slight
indeed. Inference has probably had not a little to do with the
origin of those traditions ; in other words, they are more largely
transmitted *inferences* and transmitted *reports* than they are
transmitted *testimony*.

In digging a trench, 5 feet deep, for the pipes connecting
with the Organ Motor, we came upon human remains close
against the easterly foundation wall of the transept which forms
the Organ Chamber ; but by slightly altering the direction of
the trench, were enabled to leave them undisturbed.

In explanation of the finding of such remains in a part of
the grounds where no headstones or tablets appear, we were
told by a neighbor well advanced in years, a descendant of the
Johnson family named as Church officers in the records, that
some portion of the land had been used as a burial ground prior
to its purchase for the church in 1747.

The final paragraph of the " Notes" from which the preceding " extracts" have been taken is as follows :—

" The Corner Stone of this edifice is laid in the absence of
" the Bishop, under the direction of the Rector, this 22nd day
" of August, A. D. 1861."

The ceremony of the laying of the Corner Stone is thus described by a correspondent of the " Church Journal," (New York.)

" The clergy present on this interesting occasion were the
" Rev. C. B. Ellsworth, Rector, the Rev. E. F. Edwards
" of the neighboring parish of Cold Spring Harbor, the Rev.
" E. K. Fowler of Monticello, the Rev. W. A. W. Maybin, of
" Williamsburgh, the Rev. J. H. Williams, of Dobbs Ferry, and
" the Rev. Wm. G. Farrington, of New York,— the last four
" being former rectors of the parish.

" The service used was that appointed by Bishop Hobart,
" and the stone was laid, in the absence of the Bishop of the
" Diocese, by the Rev. Mr. Fowler, who began his ministry
" here about forty years ago. All the clergy were in surplices,
" and participated in the service. The address by the Rev.
" Mr. Maybin, was excellent in matter and style, and deeply
" stirred the hearts of all present."

Communication on Old St. John's

By the Rev. Richard B. Post.

(RECEIVED THROUGH MISS NINA PRIME, JAN. 7, 1888.)

"The picture brought back to me so many memories. It
"lacked one thing associated with the old church, namely, the
"old red cedar-wood bier, which used to stand just opposite the
"South porch, with "1779" carved in rude figures upon one
"side, and upon this bier we youngsters used to sit before ser-
"vice, watching the various members of the congregation as
"they walked up the yard. Then that South Porch, or Vestry
"room, as it was afterwards made; in it we ate our lunch when
"busy dressing the church, at Christmas, *i. e.* after the Rev.
"Mr. McLeod took charge of the parish; for before that we
"knew no better than not only to eat it in the church, but also
"to warm various things on the church stove. Then there
"was the old square pew in the northwest corner of the church,
"which my father occupied, in the middle of which was a
"square table, having between the four legs a few inches from
"the floor, a piece corresponding with the top, on which I used
"to crawl at the beginning of the sermon, and sweetly sleep
"the droning time away. Those were the days when they
"had a "two-decker" on the North side of the building, with
"reading desk below and pulpit above, and a great sounding
"board directly over the latter, and I used to speculate on the
"chances and consequences if the fastenings of this ponderous

" thing should give way during the sermon. At the Commu-
" nion Office the clergyman walked to the East end where the
" altar was. Afterwards the interior was changed. The
" square pews, except those of Rhinelander and Cambreling,
" were taken away, and ordinary seats put in. The "two-
" decker" came down, and a gallery was put up at the west
" end, and an organ placed therein. Then the Choir took pos-
" session, and the Canticles began to be chanted. And there
" was a boy who used to sit in the gallery and assist in the
" singing, and during the sermon I am afraid was not always
" so attentive as he might have been. Whether this boy did
" it, or some of his companions, or both, I do not remember,
" but I know that people sitting under the gallery would more
" or less often be startled out of their sleep by various sub-
" stances falling on their heads, but the upward glance re-
" vealed not whence they came. I do not remember ever hear-
" ing that boy or the others being told much about the rever-
" ence to be shown in the House of God. Not so much as
" other boys have been told and observed. These are among
" many other recollections the picture brought forth, among
" which is one of the old sea captain who, in the absence of the
" choir, would start the hymn, giving out the name of the
" tune first; and then, in the afternoon, stating in a voice in
" which the main-top might have been hailed " We'll sing the
" same tunes we sung this mornin'!" Outside, in the grave-
" yard were the old stones, two dating "1749," and another
" with a hole through the middle of it made by a six-pound
" cannon-ball, and behind which tradition said a man was
" killed."

" And now the old church is gone. None of the clergy
" who were in charge of it as I first remember it are alive, and
" but few of the people who worshipped there.

" In the days of the square pews, the entrance was at the
" south porch. In the alterations which swept them away,
" that was made a vestry room, and a new entrance was made
" at the west end.

" Three of those who ministered there after the interior
" changes are still alive :—Dr. Hall, Dr. Farrington and Mr.
" Ellsworth."

The Rev. C. B. Ellsworth departed this life in 1891.

At the date of the writing of the foregoing note, Rev. J.
H. Williams was also in this life, and the Rev. Wm. J. Lynd
still survives.—(Ed.)

Extracts.

Extracts.

FROM A FOUR-PAGE PAPER CALLED "THE SPIRIT OF THE
FAIR." PUBLISHED AND SOLD AT A LADIES' FAIR,
SEP. 3RD. 1844, FOR A "PARSONAGE FUND."

1. From an Address to Our Patrons.

* * * *

Erected on yon summit stands
A sacred fane— whose age demands
  Our best and largest care;
'Twas reared by hearts that understood
Religion is the greatest good,
  And now its glories share!

Thus pure devotion shows its sway,
Thus works of love true faith display,
  Unto this present hour;
Nor can the bright memorial cease
In us the like desire t' increase
  Whilst godliness hath power.

* * * *

Ah! never shall our CHURCH decay!
Time may, indeed, devour its prey,
  Her outward form deface:
Yet, Phœnix-like, will she arise,
And towering o'er her enemies,
  Subdue proud Edom's race!

There, through the bless'd REDEEMERS'
    name,
Did mighty men of God proclaim
  The counsel of His will;
There GREATON -there our SEABURYS too
Goliaths were they! to pursue
  Their mission to fulfil.

There HOBART— venerable man !
And our own loved DIOCESAN
  Brave champion of the Cross !

And RUDD—a name remembered well,
Nor less esteemed—of JESUS tell
  And how He died for us !

Then bless, O HEAVENLY FATHER, bless
The cause of truth and righteousness
  Which we, in CHRIST's name, plead ;

That they who labor for our good,
May be supplied with daily food,
  Nor 'mong us suffer need.

     * * * *

The Ladies' Fair.

From a humorous description, in verse, (whose feet and
rhymes occasionally need to be tested with not too fastidious
ear, or, as regards the former, scanned with no critical eye,)
the following extracts are made, 1st, because they make pleas-
ant mention of workers whose lives and personalities may still
be happily remembered, and secondly, because in the concluding
stanzas the good ladies show that while holding a " Fair " as a
means of raising money for church purposes they are fully sensible of the lack of fitness and dignity in such methods, and in
words that we hope will commend themselves to the hearts and
consciences of our people they most eloquently preach the " more
excellent way."

     * * * *

" See there is Mrs. Marcus yonder
Who o'er your kindness oft will ponder,
There's Mrs. Rhinelander who, no less

The Ladies' Fair.

Will gratefully her thanks express
For all donations you may give her
For she's the Lady Treasurer.
There's Mrs. Stout who—happy name
Has gained at Fairs a deathless fame,—
As Secretary, will record
Whate'er your willing purse affords
There's Mrs. Cambreling who will too,
Appreciate whate'er you may do,
And with her very smile contribute
Pleasure around her to distribute.
There's Mrs. Higbee—bless her soul—
Who doth the hearts of all control,
Will with all readiness receive
As much as you're disposed to give;
There's Mrs. Thurston—light and airy,
Flitting about you like a Fairy,—
With Mrs. Hawthorn—kind as ever,
Who from her friend we will not sever,
That will to all your wants attend
And sundry good things recommend.
And there is Mrs. Harrison
Who, though from Princeton, *is* our great gun

      *   *   *   *

Nor are these all—there's Mrs. Post.
Who of her charms, indeed, may boast;
And also Mrs. Schermerhorn
For love itself and goodness born!
There's Mrs. Conklin—Mrs. Ray—
Who each have borne their part to-day;
There's Mrs. Williams—with her daughter,
Whose face beams forth with mirth and laugh-
    ter;
And Mrs. Rowell, who as well
Can form her flowers, out of shell
As any artist e'er attempted—
Titian alone, perhaps, excepted!
And now, beside the married dames.
We may recite some other names
The Misses Renwick, and Miss Barnwell,
Whose every glance doth their true worth tell!
These for our Fair have labored far more

Than we, in verse, can well recount o'er.
There's Miss Eliza Scudder, who
Will send you all a *billet-doux* —
Whose zeal and labor in the cause
Demand our praise and your applause,
And there (Miss Kate not to adduce—)
Miss Mary Post — Miss Susan House-
Who far more diligent than many
We think will yet compare with any !
There's Miss Cornelia Scudder too
Whom beaux from far and near would woo,
And there's Miss Smith, and Miss Van Arsdale
Whose charms to please can never fail !

    * * * *

" The Ladies' Fair- ah ! fair indeed,
When we are thus compelled to plead
E'en for the best and holiest cause
The Church of Christ :- and that because
Men do not feel, as feel they ought,
But, faithless stewards, must be bought ;
Entrapped by female charms and beauty
To do what well they know, their duty !
Yet how much fairer would it be,
Could we but raise your piety
By means which move and touch the heart,
And thus persuade you to impart
Freely as God hath prospered you !
Then should we not this course pursue !
Soon may the happy time arrive
When we shall all our joy contrive
From doing good from love to Him
Who died our souls from death t' redeem ;
Then will the scene be fair and bright
And God in all our works delight."

    The next, and concluding, extract has both personal and
historical interest. It was written by Bishop Onderdonk for
the N. Y. " Churchman," in making record of the Consecration
of the Church, which was effected on July 9th, 1839.

" This church is one of the oldest churches in the diocese,
" having been built probably—for there is singular uncertainty
" respecting its true history—more than a century ago ; and of
" course long before we had bishops in this country. At the
" time of its erection, therefore, it was not consecrated. Having
" been for many years in a very neglected condition, and but
" rarely opened for divine service, a few zealous and enterpris-
" ing members of the Church, recently moving into the Parish,
" determined upon its thorough repair. This having been ac-
" complished, its consecration was asked of the Bishop of the
" Diocese, and effected as above detailed. In the appointment
" of the clergymen—father and son—for the services of the
" desk, reference was had by the Bishop to the past history of
" the parish—they having both been, at different times, in its
" pastoral charge. The grandfather of the elder—the Rev.
" Samuel Seabury, father of Bishop Seabury, had this church
" included in his mission as a missionary of the Venerable So-
" ciety in England for Propagating the Gospel in Foreign Parts.
" His son, the bishop, officiated there, before his ordination, as
" a Catechist and Lay Reader of that Society, and probably
" afterwards occasionally, in his clerical capacity, while settled
" at Jamaica. Thus has that ancient building been supplied
" with services by four successive generations of the same fam-
" ily."

Deeds of the Glebe.

And Communication Referring to Them.

In this paper, the Editor has collected, and arranged in
their proper order, certain copies of Deeds and Letters which
were quoted and referred to, but not in chronological sequence
or with much note of connexion, by the late Mr. Henry Lloyd
in a series of articles over the signature " A. N. Oldfell" in a
local newspaper.

To these is added an extract (numbered 3) from a letter of
the Rev. James Greaton which will show that the House and
Glebe mentioned in Mr. Lloyd's letter (numbred 4) of the year
following was *not the same* with the House and Glebe deeded
to the S. P. G. in 1764. We have at present no *positive* evidence that the instructions given by Mr. Lloyd in his letter of
1770 were actually carried out. There is *presumptive* evidence
that they were, for we know that in letters which passed between Mrs. Greaton and Mr. Lloyd subsequent to Mr. Greaton's
death in 1773, Mrs. Greaton writes as a tenant of the house and
land belonging to the church. (See Lloyd letters quoted in the
articles before referred to and lately given to the New York
Historical Society by Mrs. O. E. Schmidt.) But whether the
church wardens after the close of the Revolutionary war could
show that they, or the Society for the Propagation of the Gospel, held the deeds mentioned in the letter of 1770, this we do
not know. The deeds returned from London, and mentioned

in the letter (numbered 5) of June 1st, 1787, were those of "the Old Glebe."

1. Indenture made Aug. 21, 1764, to the Society for the Propagation of the Gospel, with proviso that Mr. Kneeland be admitted to Holy Orders and have a Mission as Minister or Rector. Being a conveyance of " five acres more or less" bounded " by the highway to the old mill dam, by land laid out for the churchyard, &c." (as given in the "Annals") By Thomas Jarvis, John Bennett, Isaiah Rogers, Zophar Rogers, Jeremiah Rogers and Samuel Allen.

Witness, WM. SMITH.

Declared before RICH'D FLOYD,

Judge.

2. Conveyance made Nov. 21, 1764, to the same, but without the proviso stated in No. 1, the same property " five " acres more or less, bounded, &c., to endow the Parish Church " called —— before mentioned to the Society for the Propaga- " tion of the Gospel in foreign parts, but in trust, and for this " special intent and purpose, that is to say, that as soon as there " shall be a Rector or Minister according to the order of the " Church of England, etc., instituted and inducted into the said " Church called Trinity Church in Huntington aforesaid, the " premises shall then be, and inure to the use of the said rec- " tor incumbent and his successors, as the Glebe land of the " said church, in fee simple forever."

Executed by Thomas Jarvis and others as before, with the addition of Henry Lloyd, and with statement of obligation of these parties and their heirs to defend the church in said holding.

Witnesses for HENRY LLOYD'S signature,

HENRY SMITH,

PASCHAL NELSON SMITH.

Witnesses for the others,

THOMAS WICKES,

ANANIAS BRUSH.

Declared by MR. LLOYD before FOSTER HUTCHINSON,

Justice.

Declared for the others before JOSEPH LEWIS,

Justice.

3. Extract from a letter of the Rev. James Greaton, at Boston, on a visit, to the S. P. G. dated August 8th, 1769.

" I flatter myself that in time a flourishing church may be " raised up there, (*i. e.* at Huntington) if the people are so hap- " py as to continue to enjoy the smiles of the Society. The " people have purchased a new glebe, with a good house, at a " cost of £344, currency, which they propose to make over to " the Society in lieu of the old glebe, which cost only £120."

4. A letter from H. Lloyd 2nd, at Boston, Oct. 1st, 1770, to Joseph Lloyd.

" Enclosed you have a deed from the proprietors of the " House and Glebe now occupied by the Rev. Mr. Greaton, at " Huntington, and my separate deed for the same to the Church " Wardens, both executed by me : one of them only to be made " use of, the other to be cancelled. The deed drawn here is

"judged safest, as in case the Society should by any change of
"government or otherwise, be dissolved, it will remain under
"the direction of the Wardens for the use of the Church, and
"cannot be alienated. Enclosed also is the Church Wardens'
"deed to the society.

"P. S.—When the deed to the society is finished you
"may send it to me, and I will forward it to my friend in Lon-
"don to be exchanged for the deeds of the Old Glebe, which is
"all that is necessary to be done under that head."

5. A letter from Henry Smith, (a son of Margaret, sister
to H. Lloyd, 2nd,) to John Lloyd, Jr. Esq., dated "Boston,
June 1st, 1787.

"*Dear Sir*:—By direction of our Uncle, Henry Lloyd,
"Esq., I enclose to you two deeds of the Old Glebe, at Hunt-
"ington, to the Society for the Propagation of the Gospel in
"foreign parts. You will please to be so good as to acknow-
"ledge the receipt of this by a line when convenient."

"Your affectionate kinsman,"

"HENRY SMITH."

The late Mr. Lloyd refers to the above (No. 5) as "an extract of a letter accompanying the document." (No. 2).

www.ingramcontent.com/pod-product-compliance
Lightning Source LLC
Chambersburg PA
CBHW032243080426
42735CB00008B/974